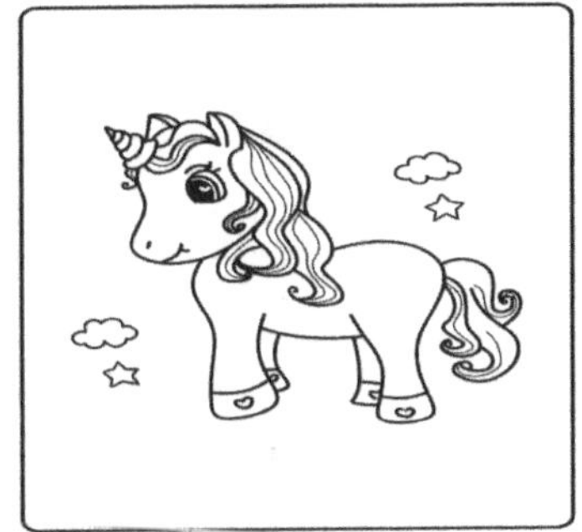

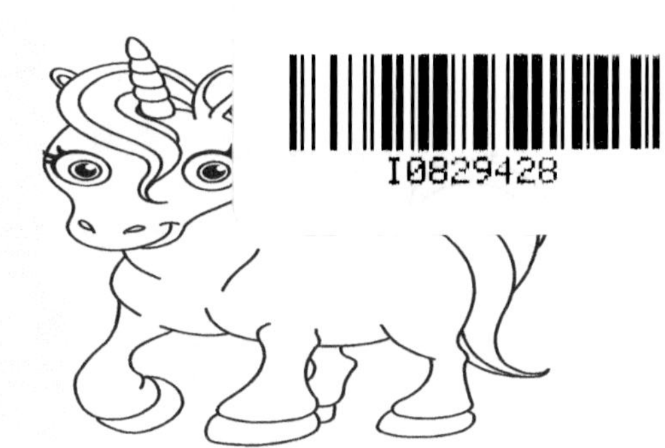

This Book Belongs to

____

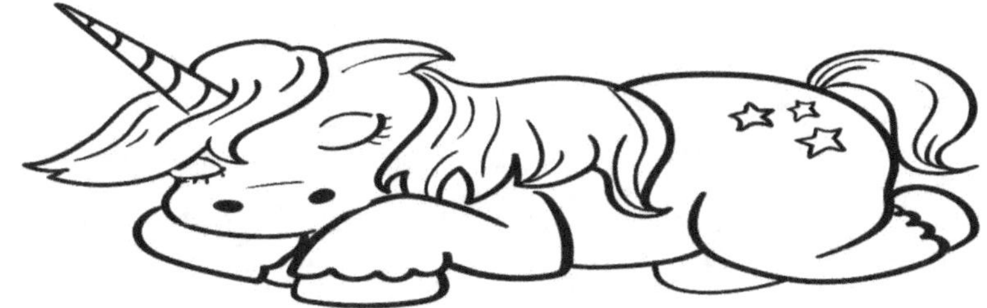

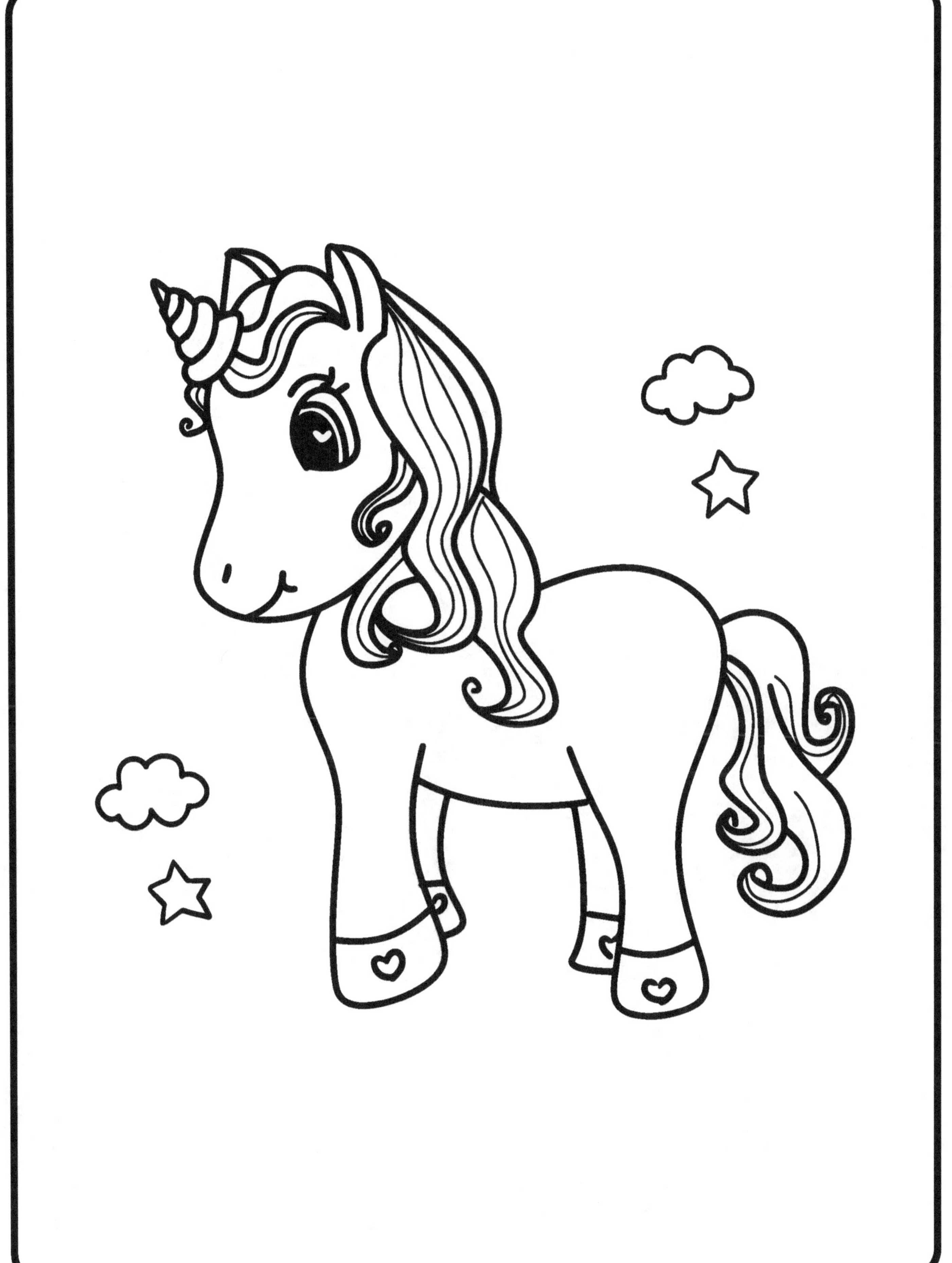

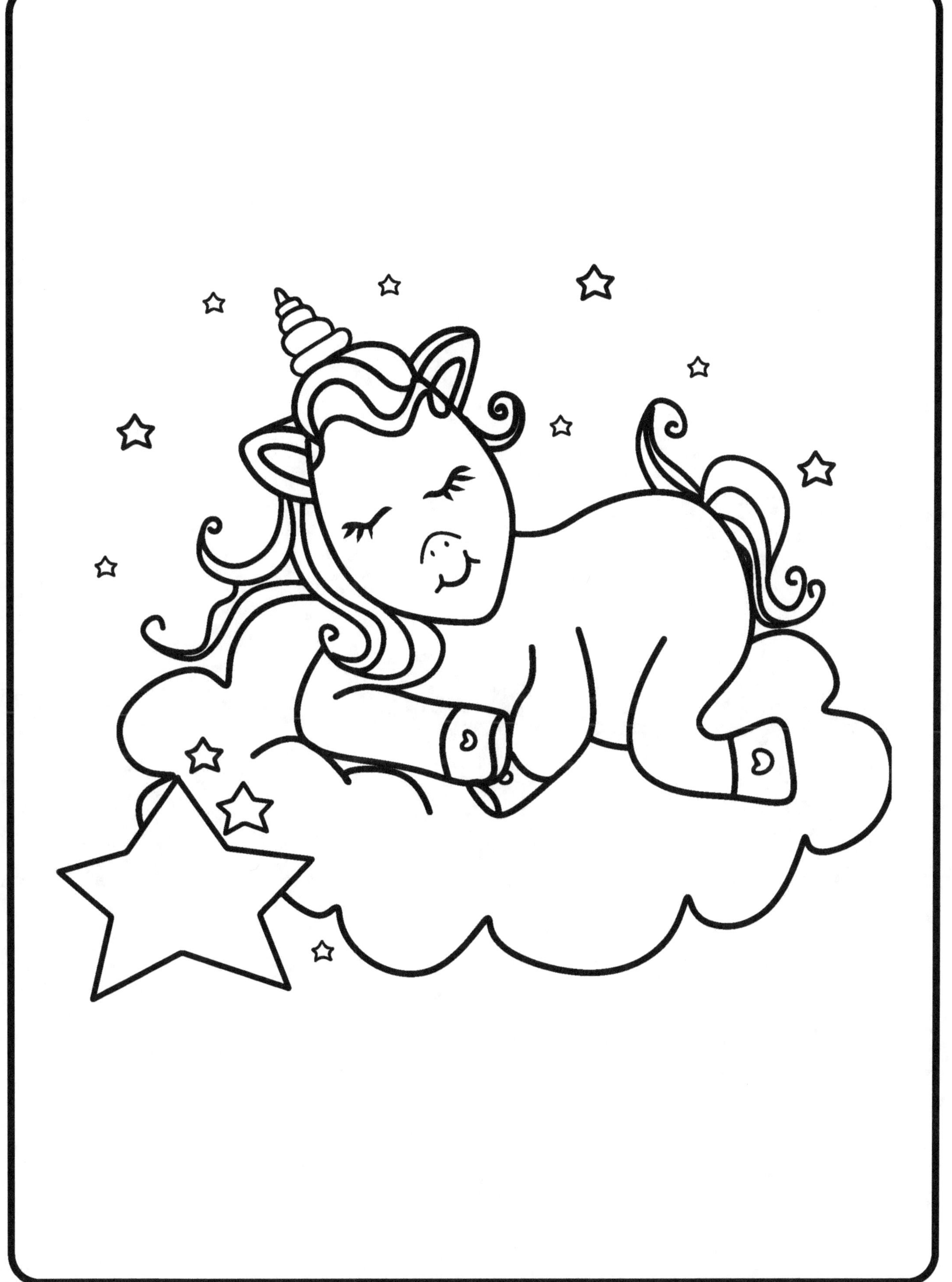

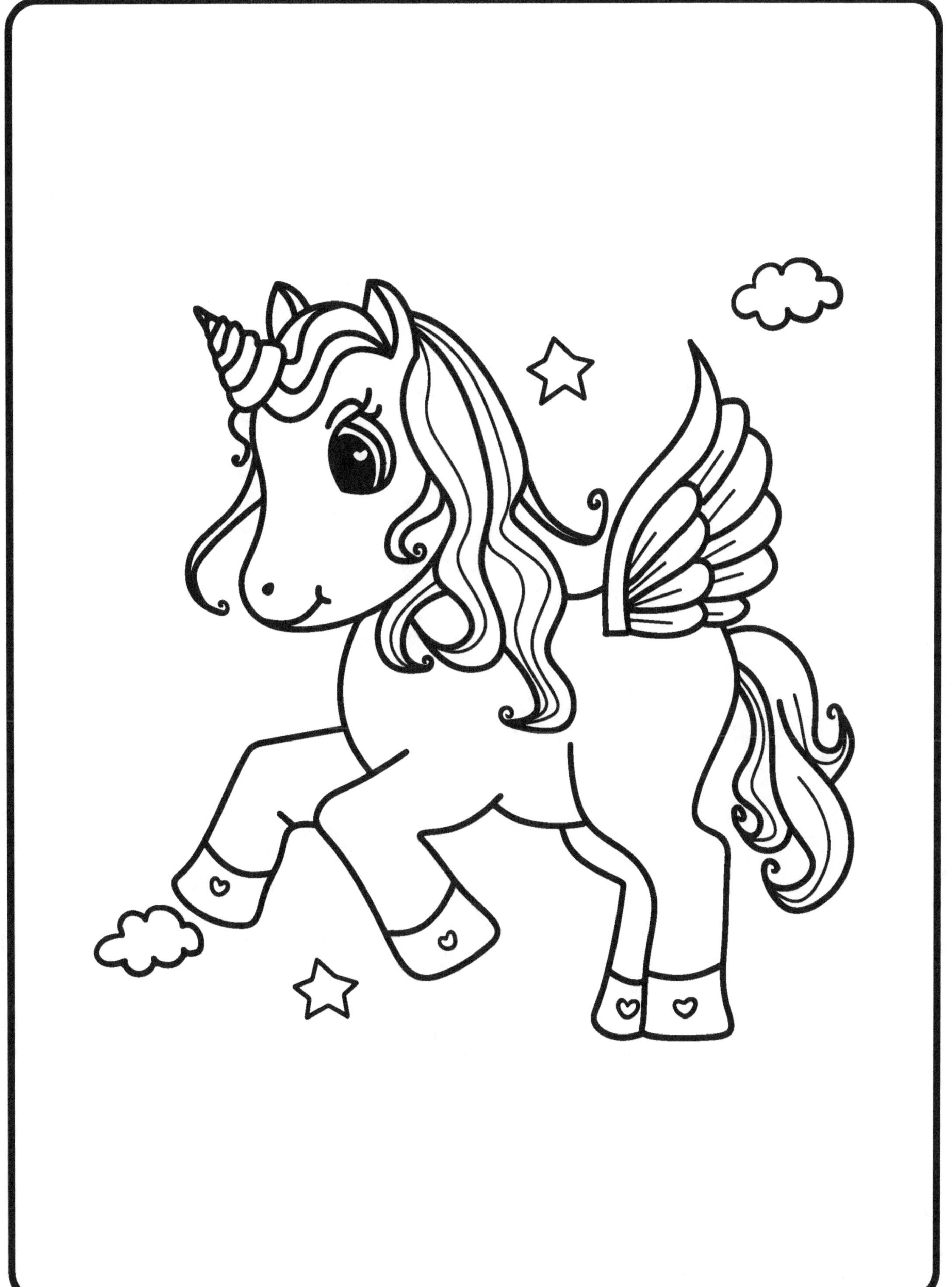

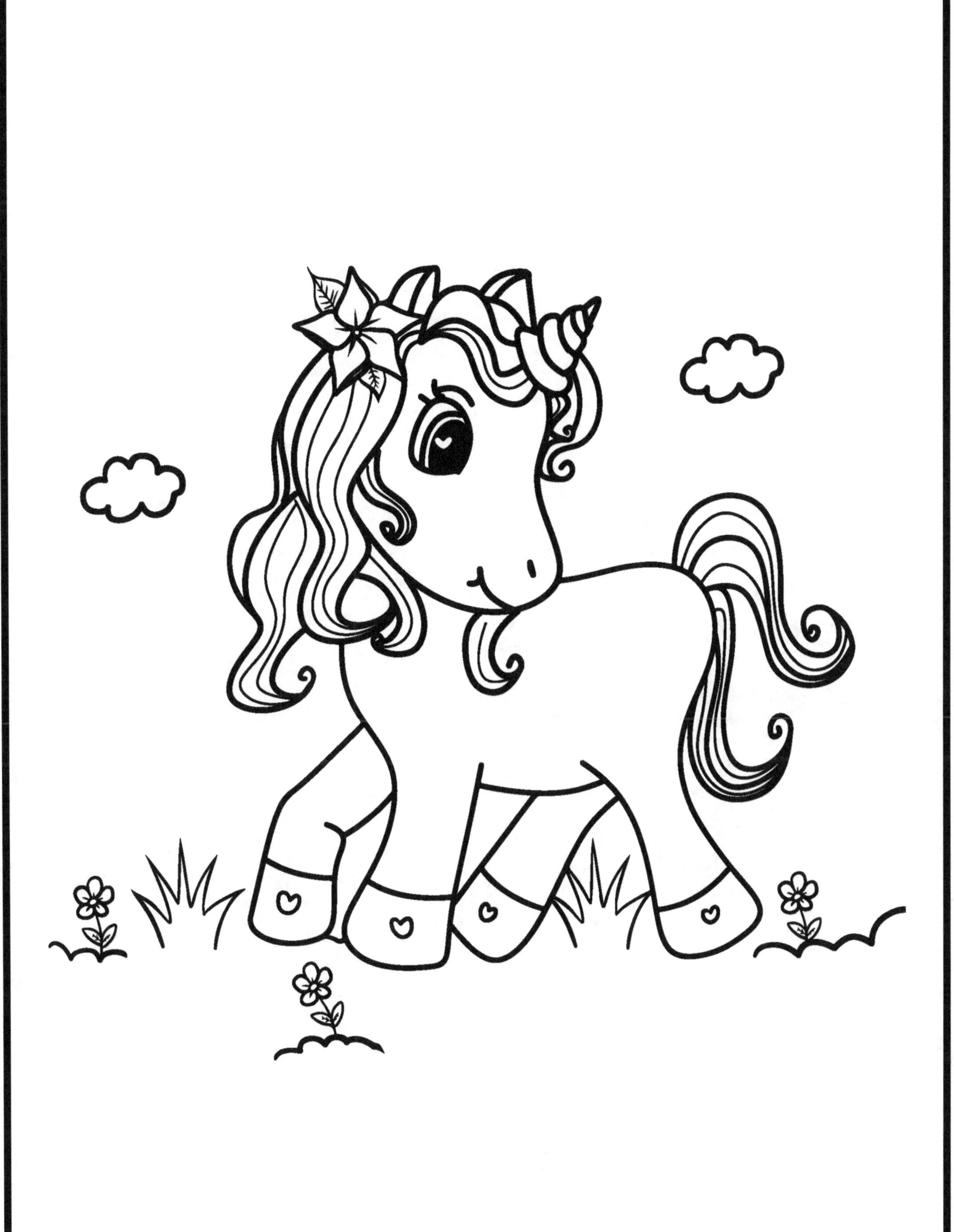

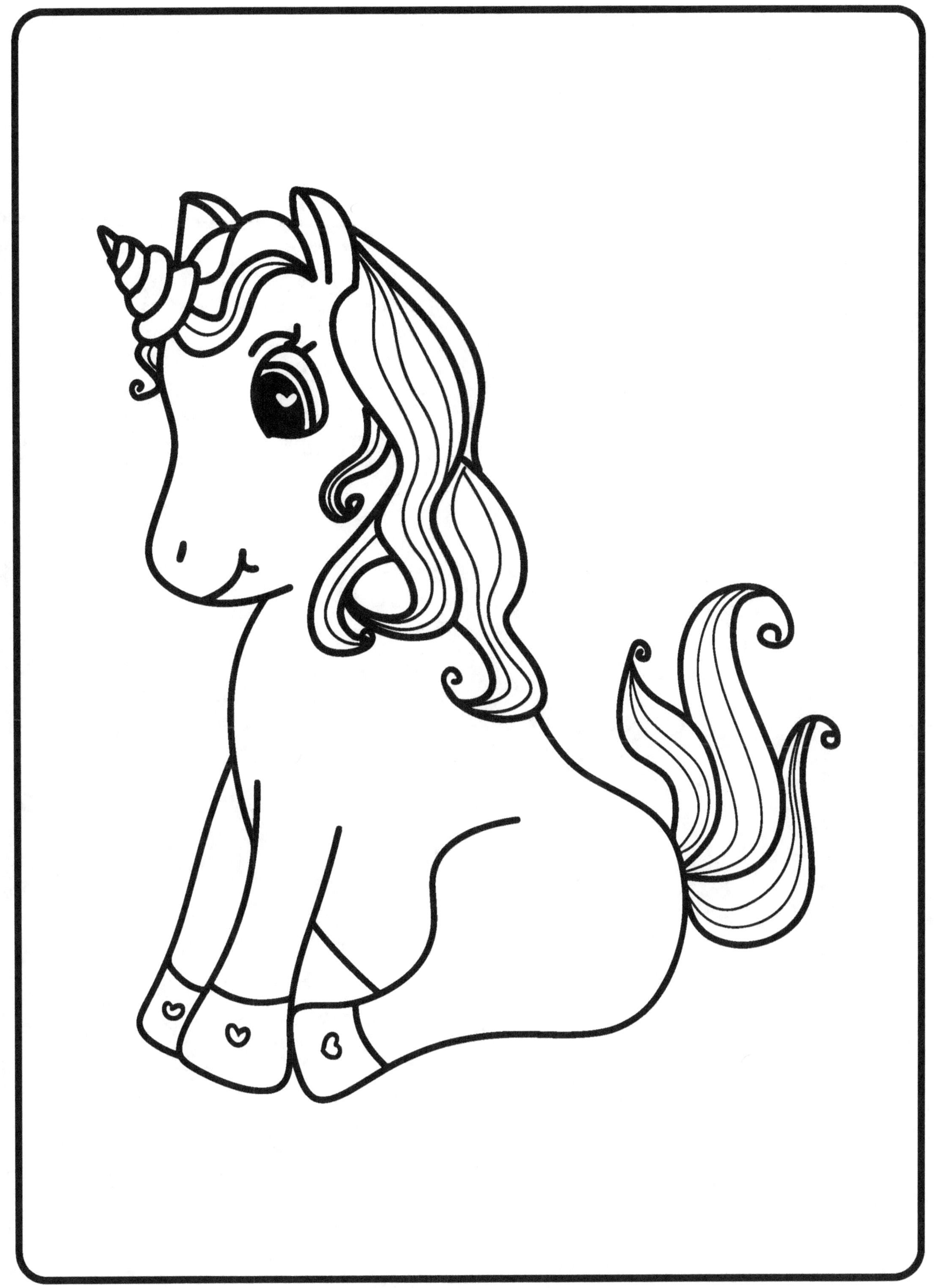

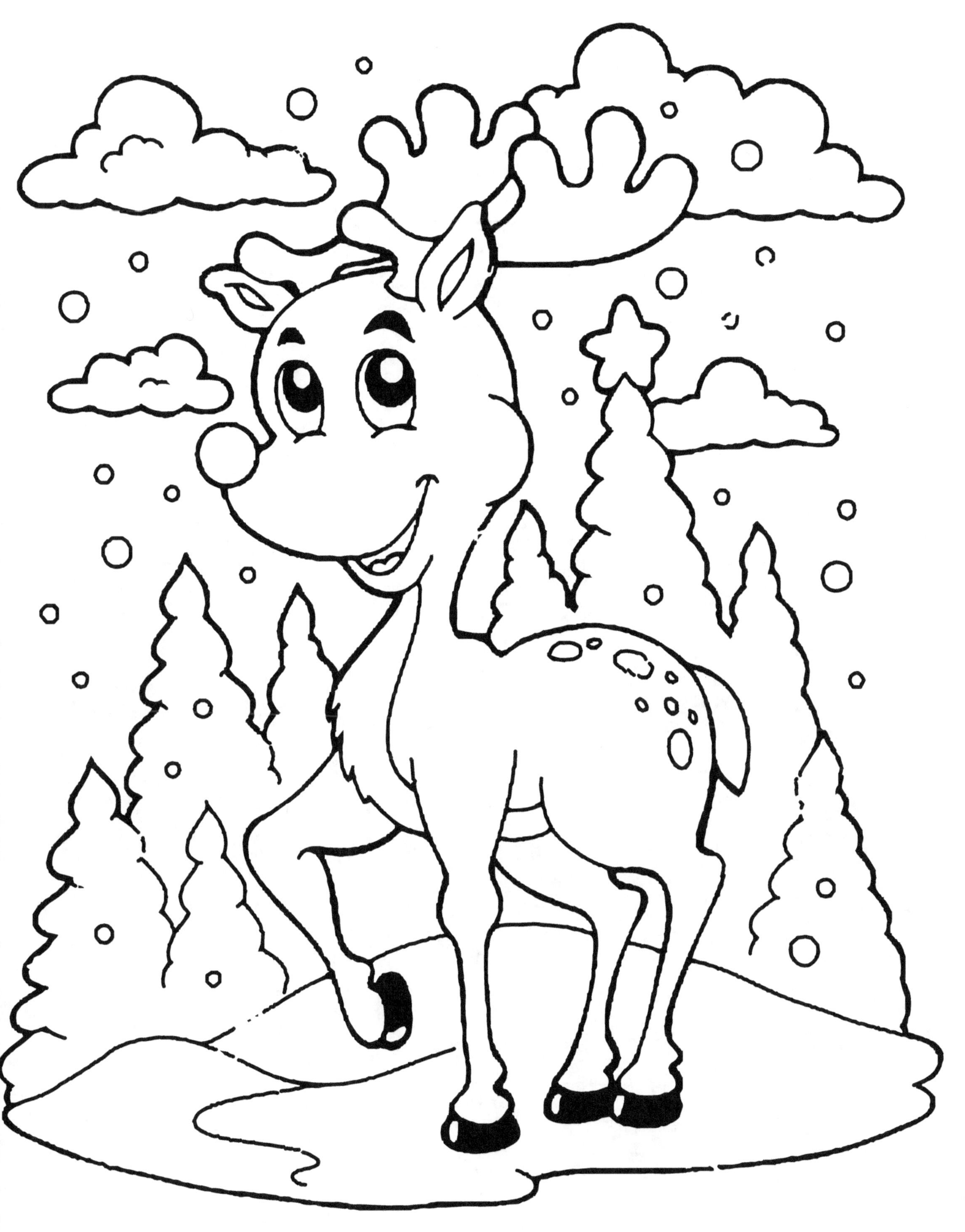

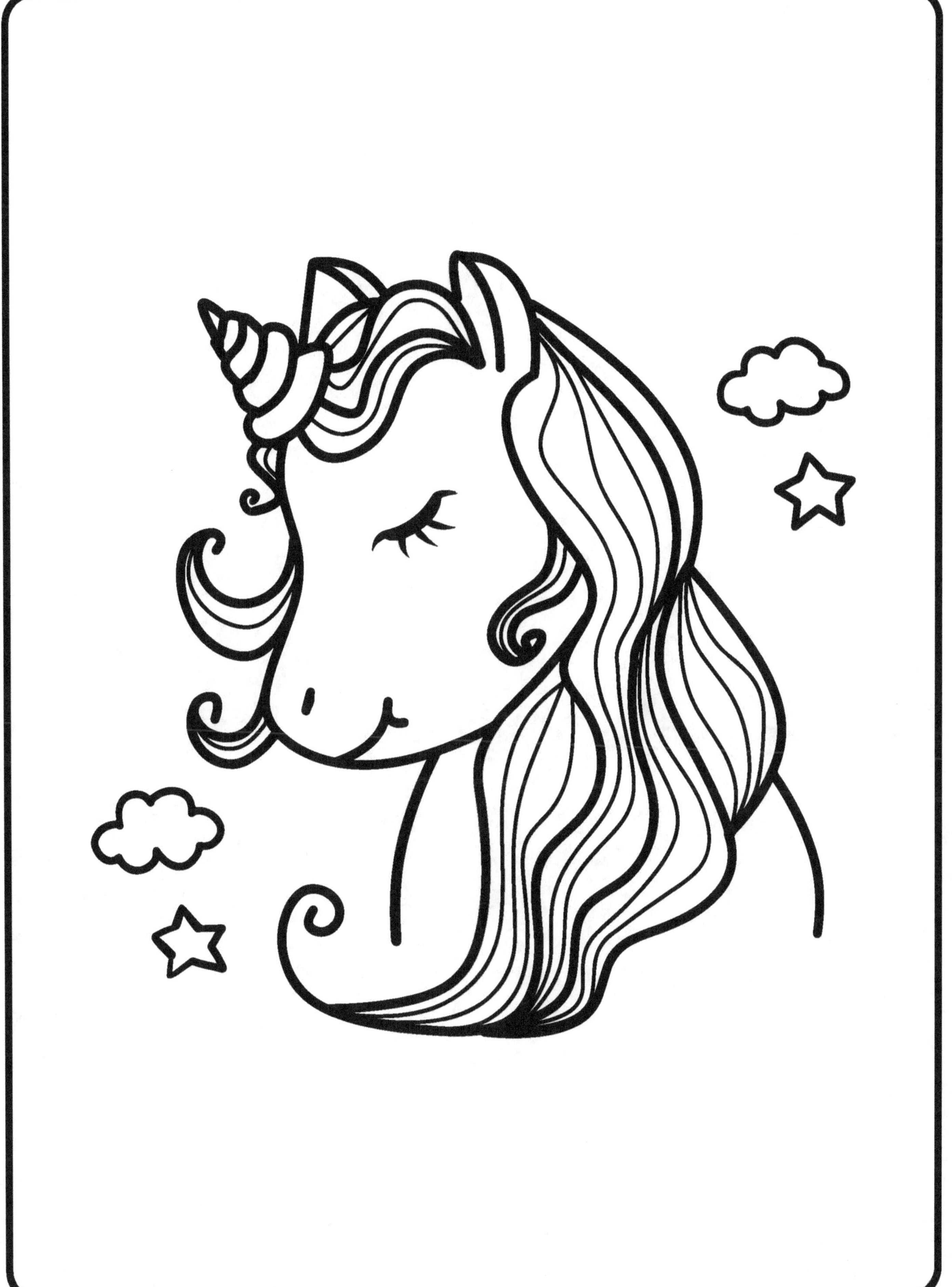

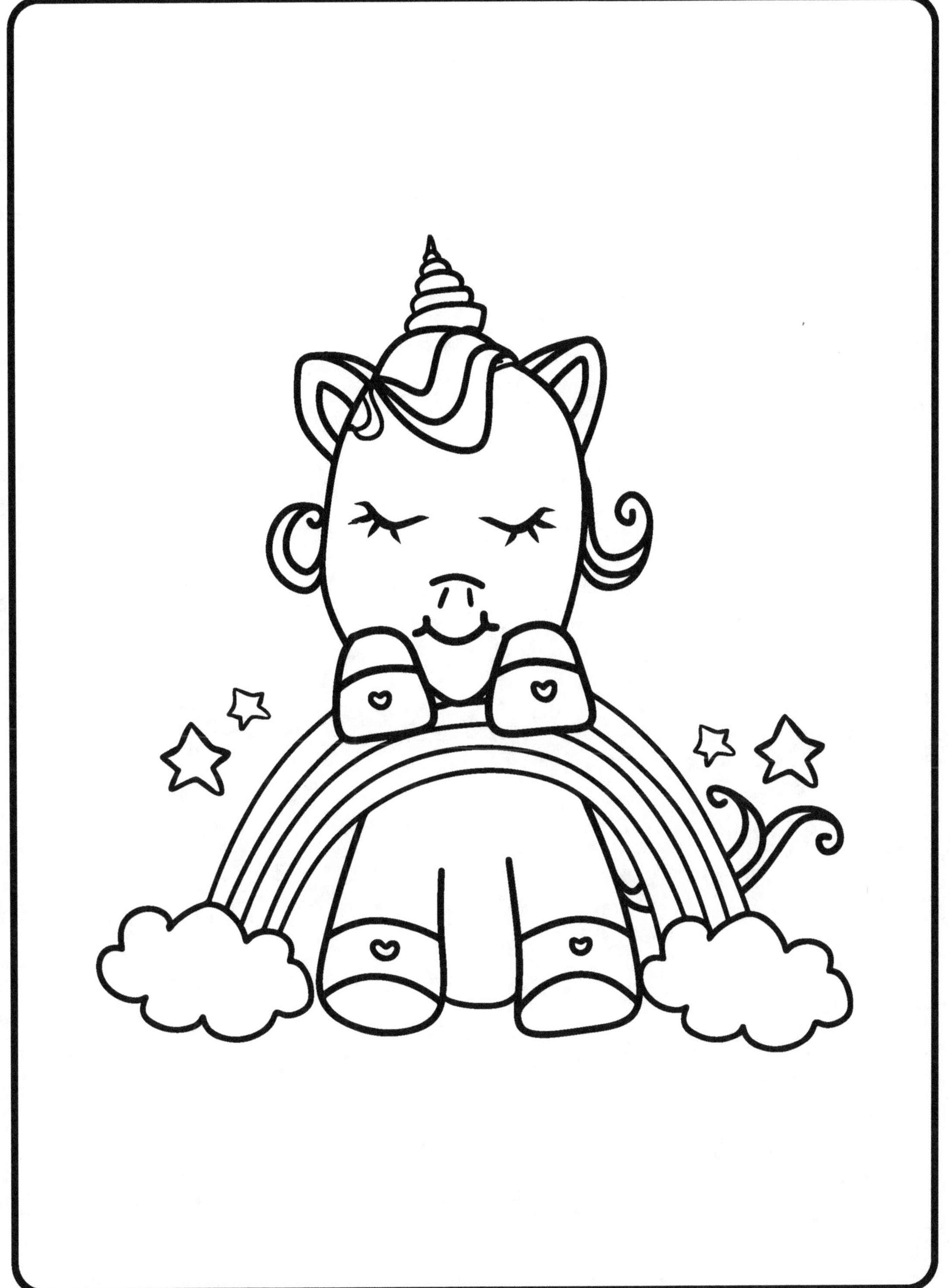

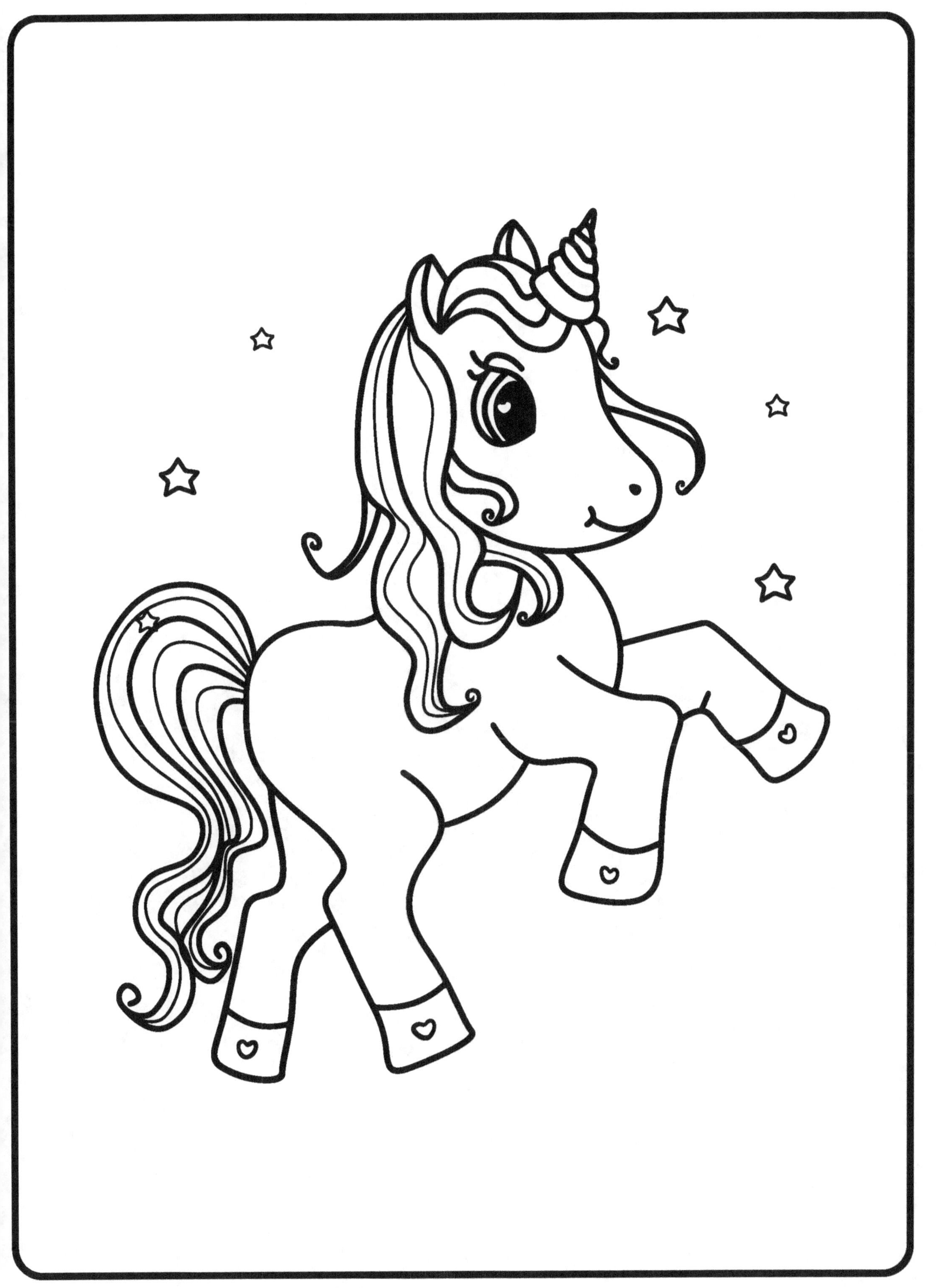

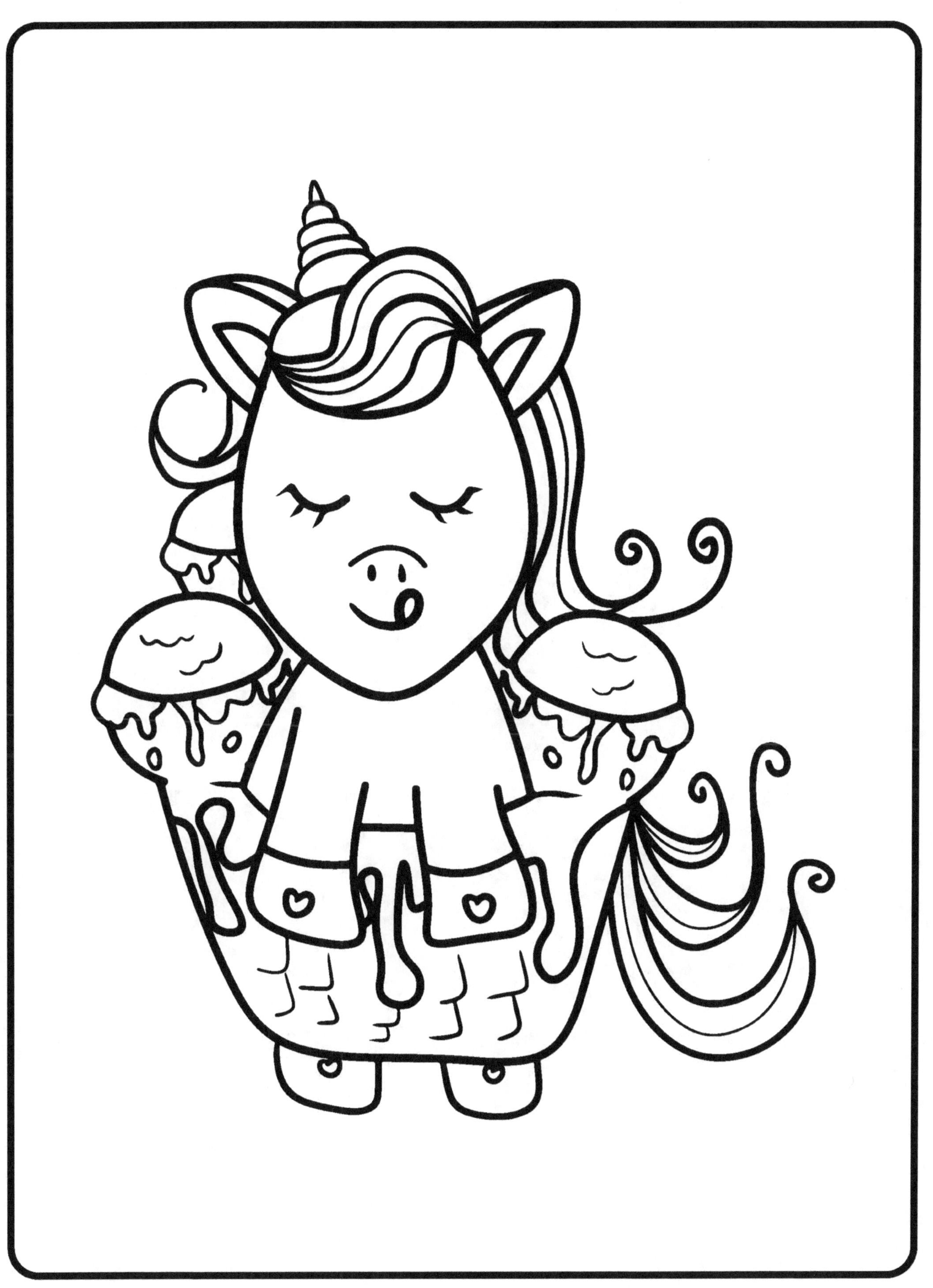

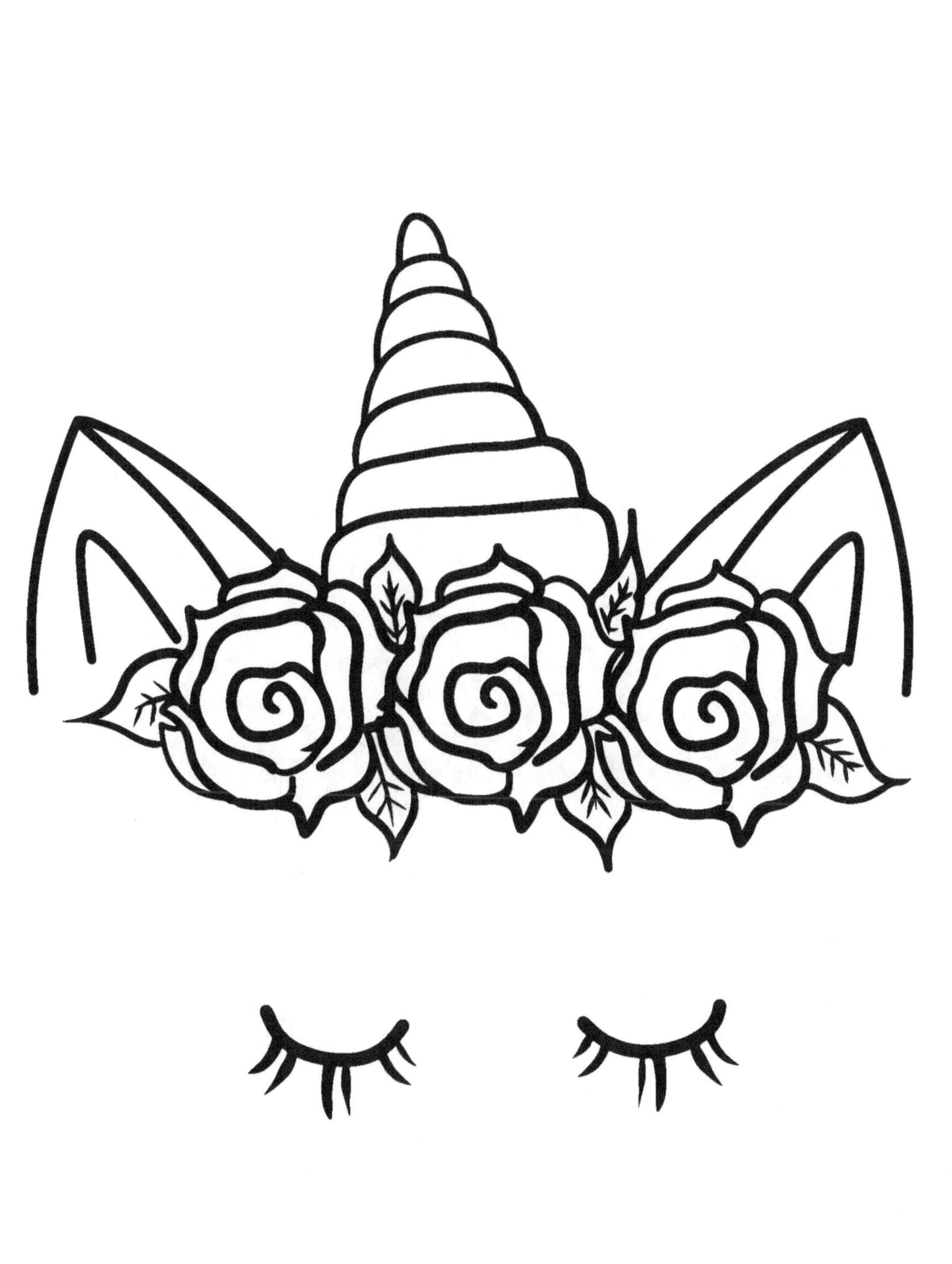

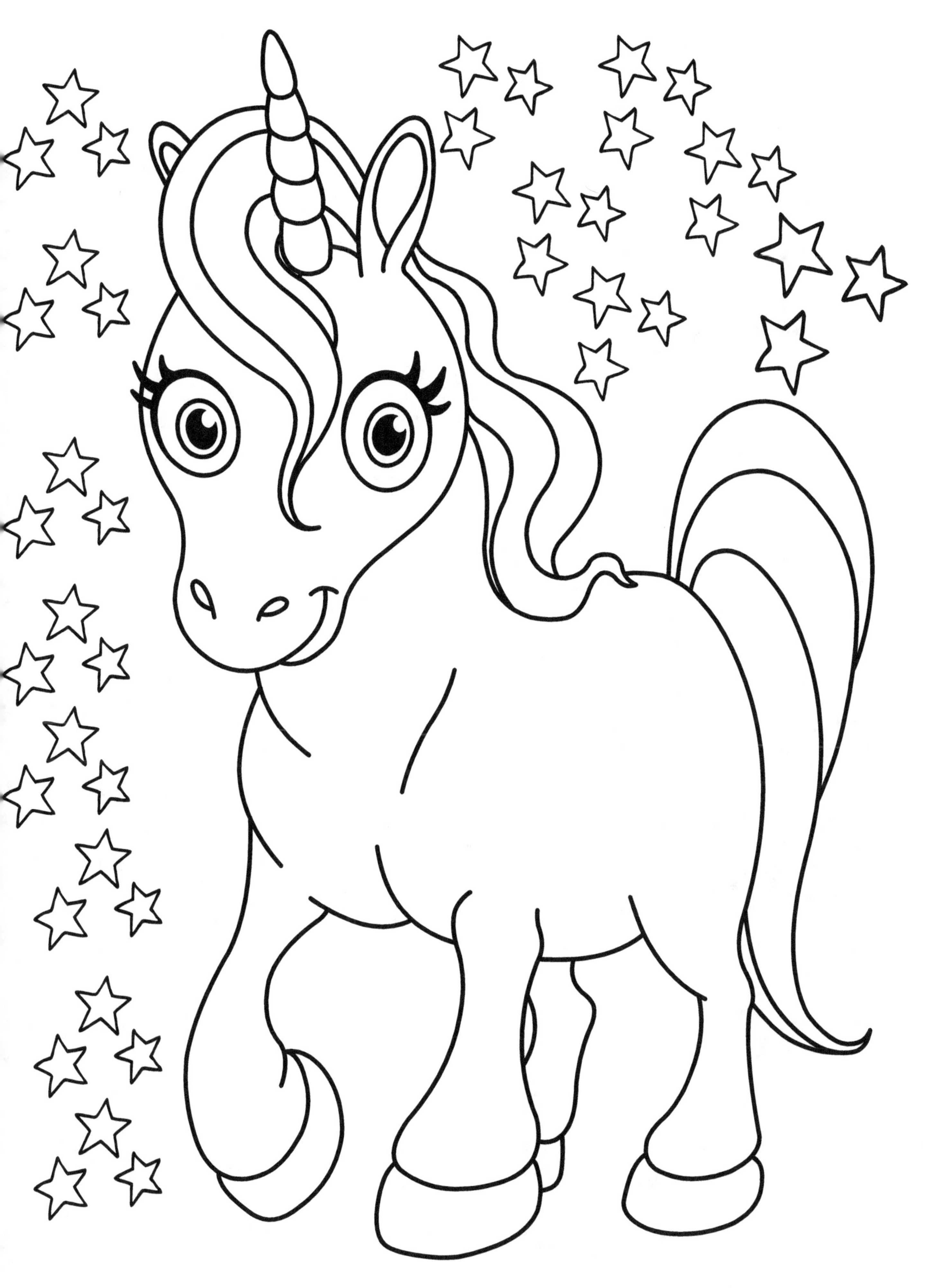

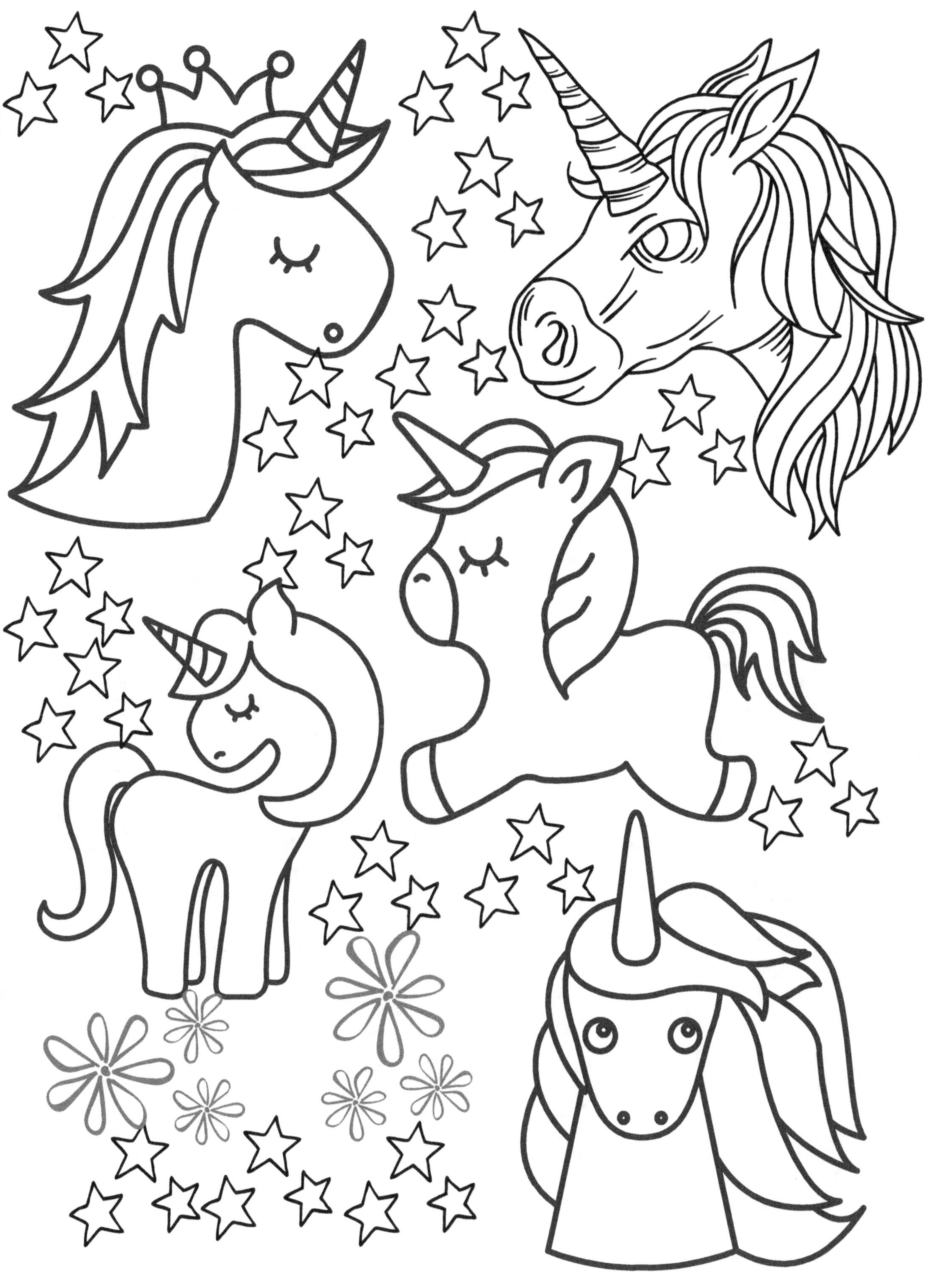

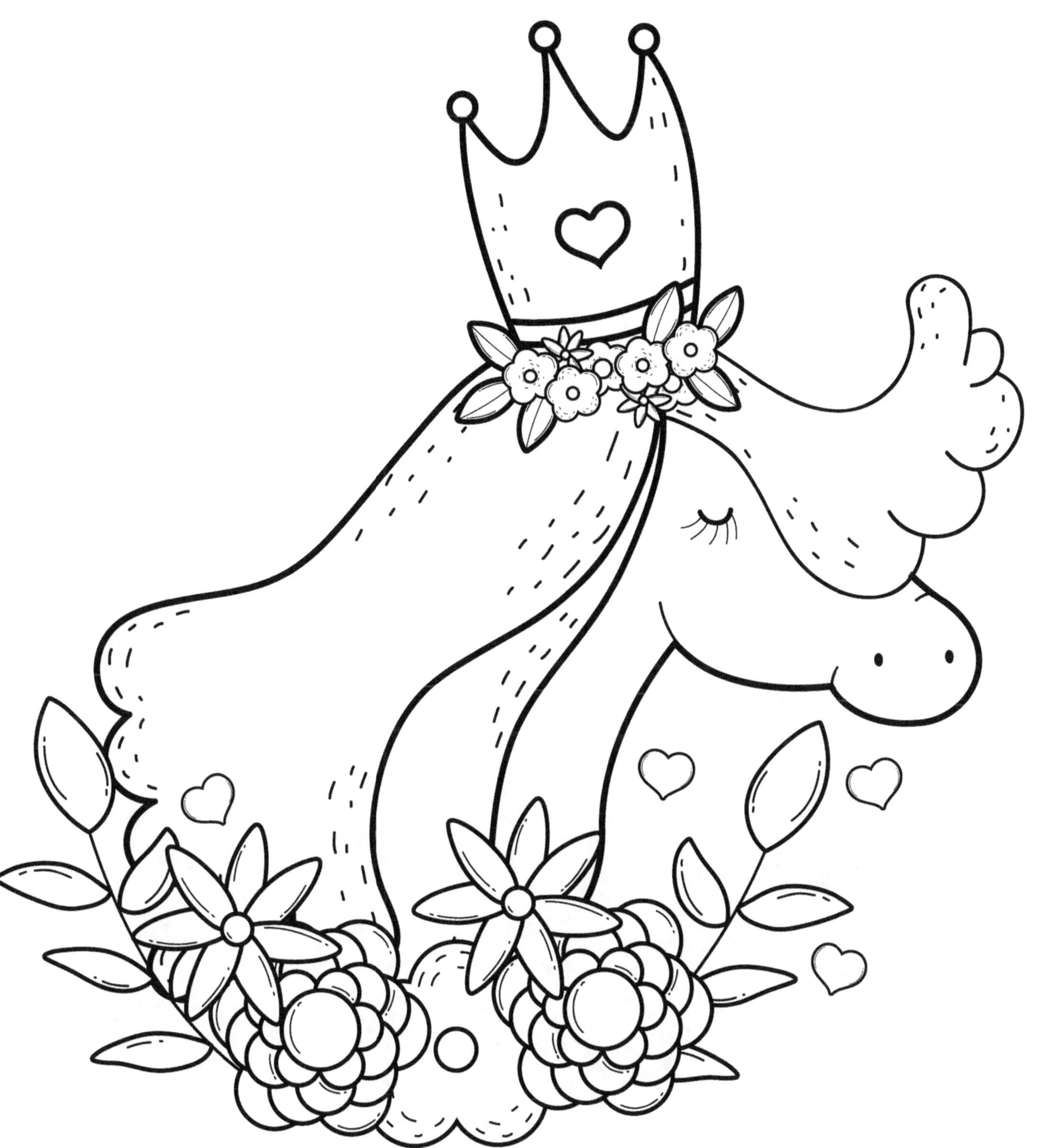

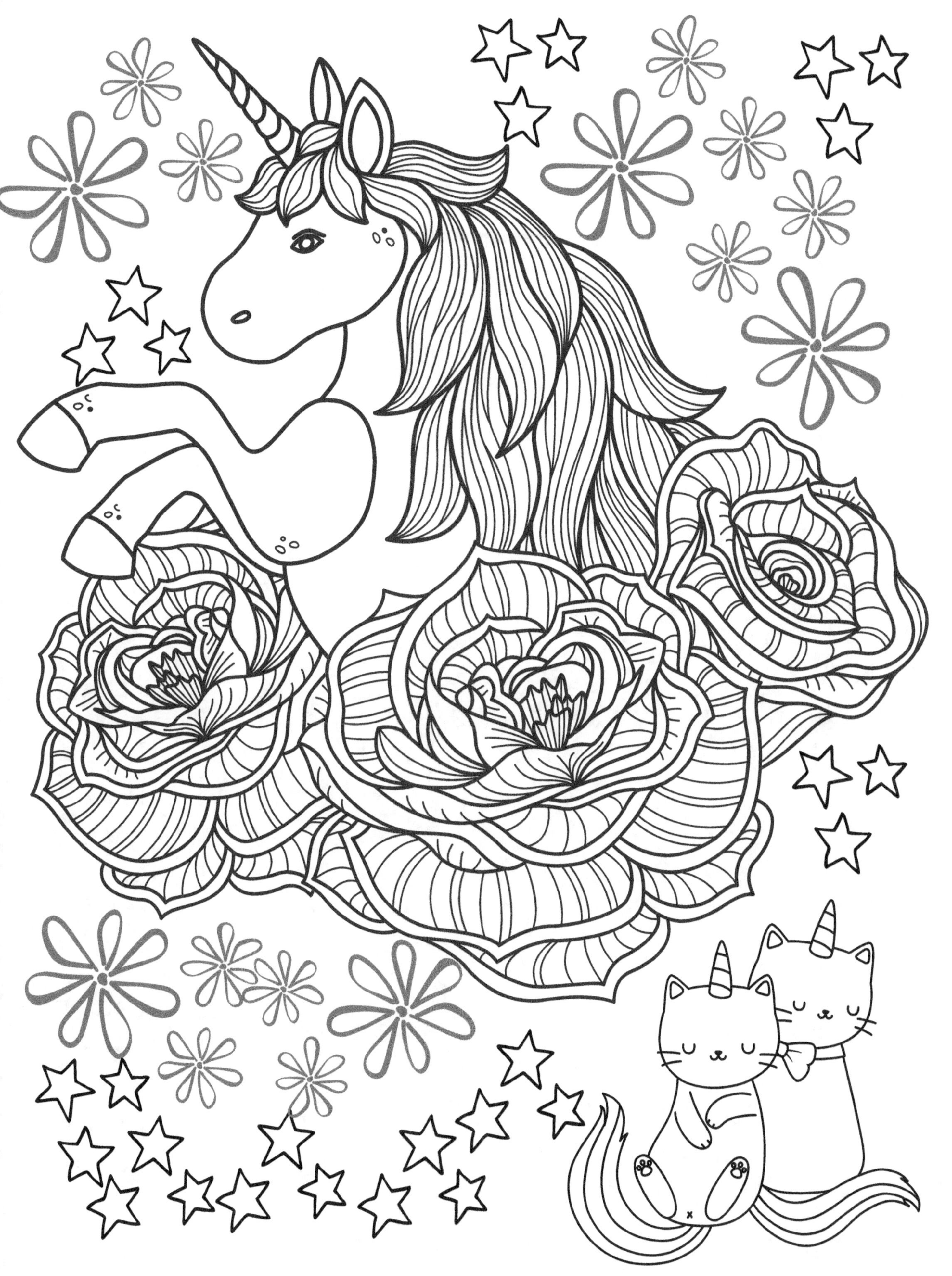

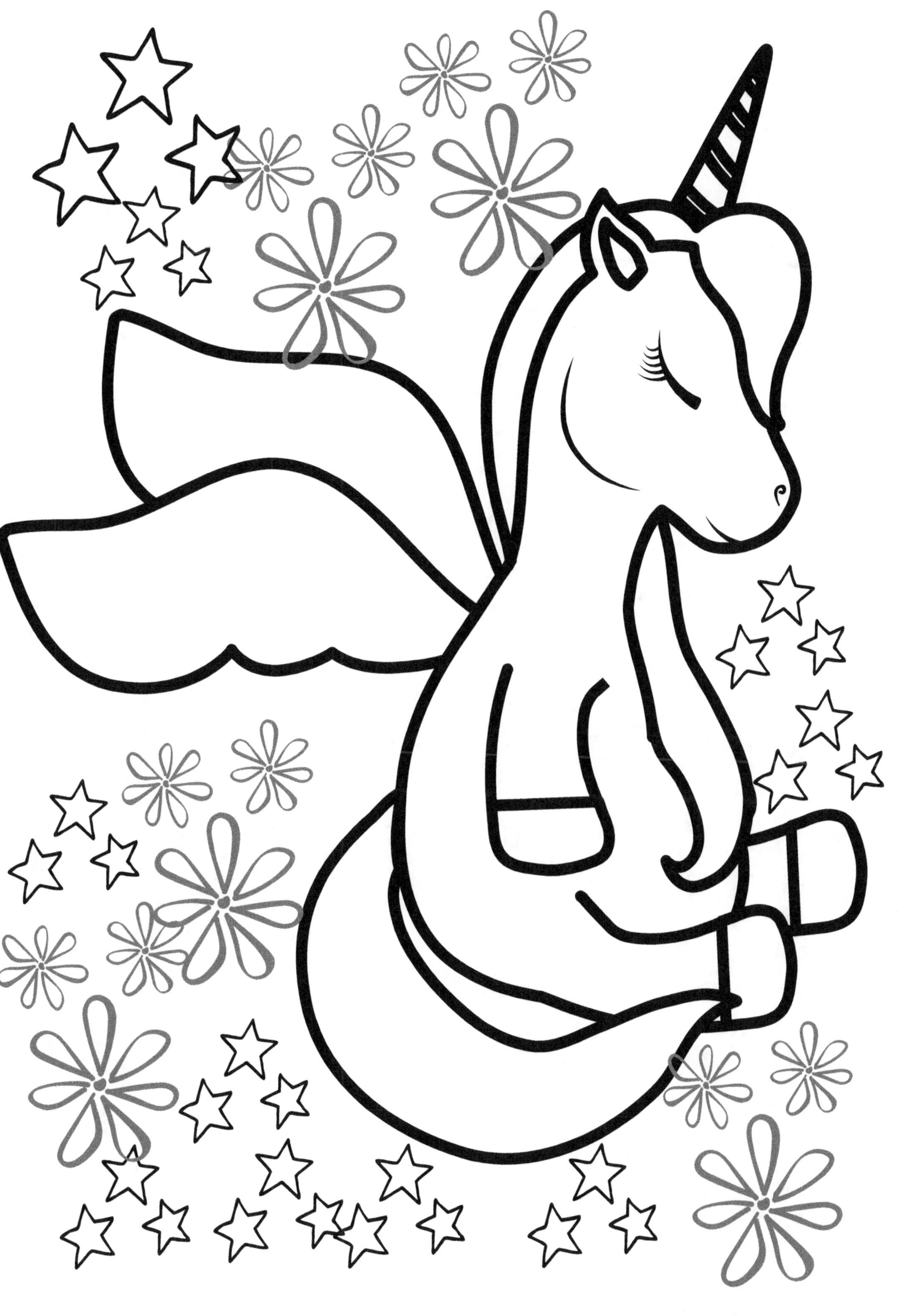

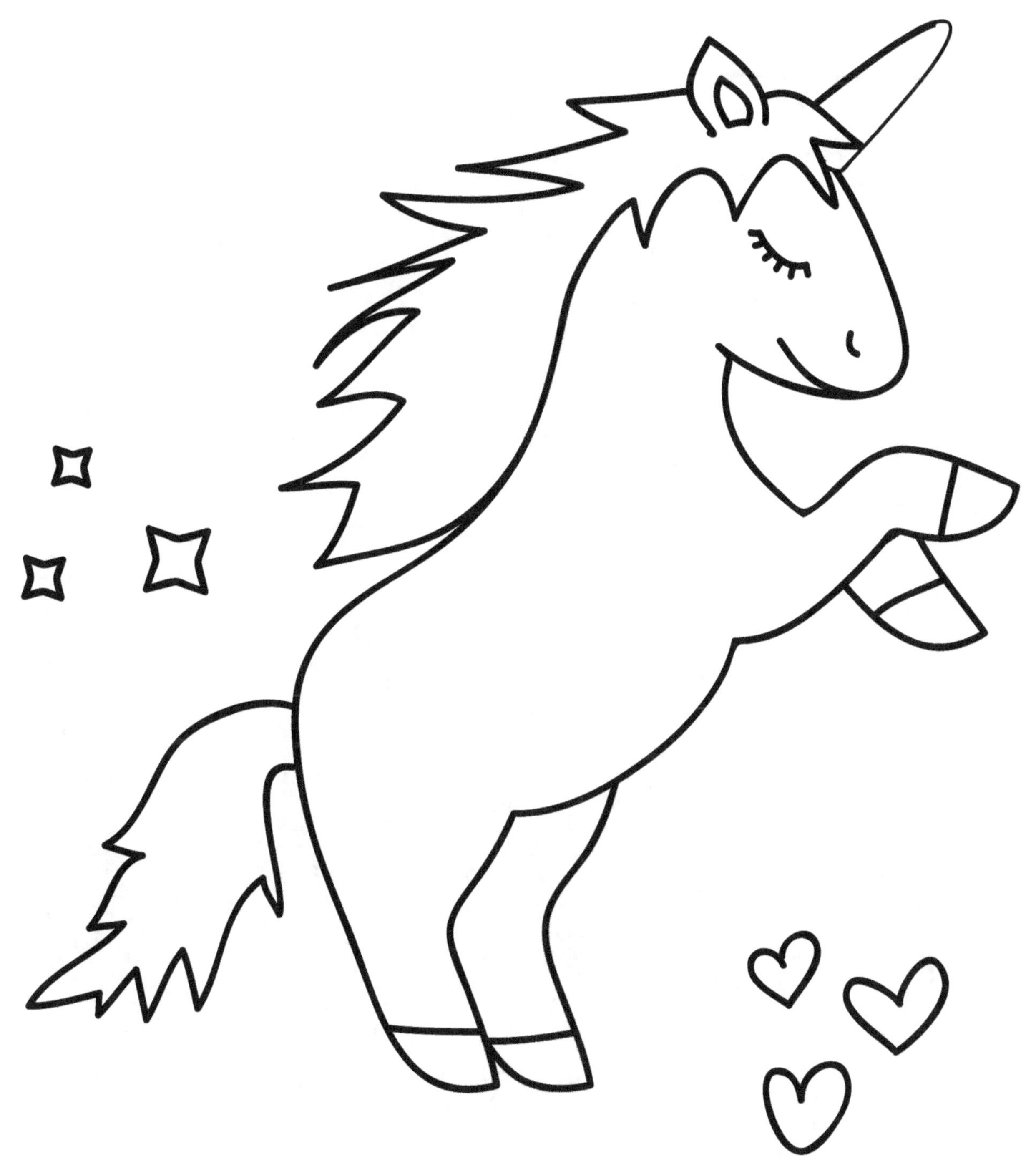

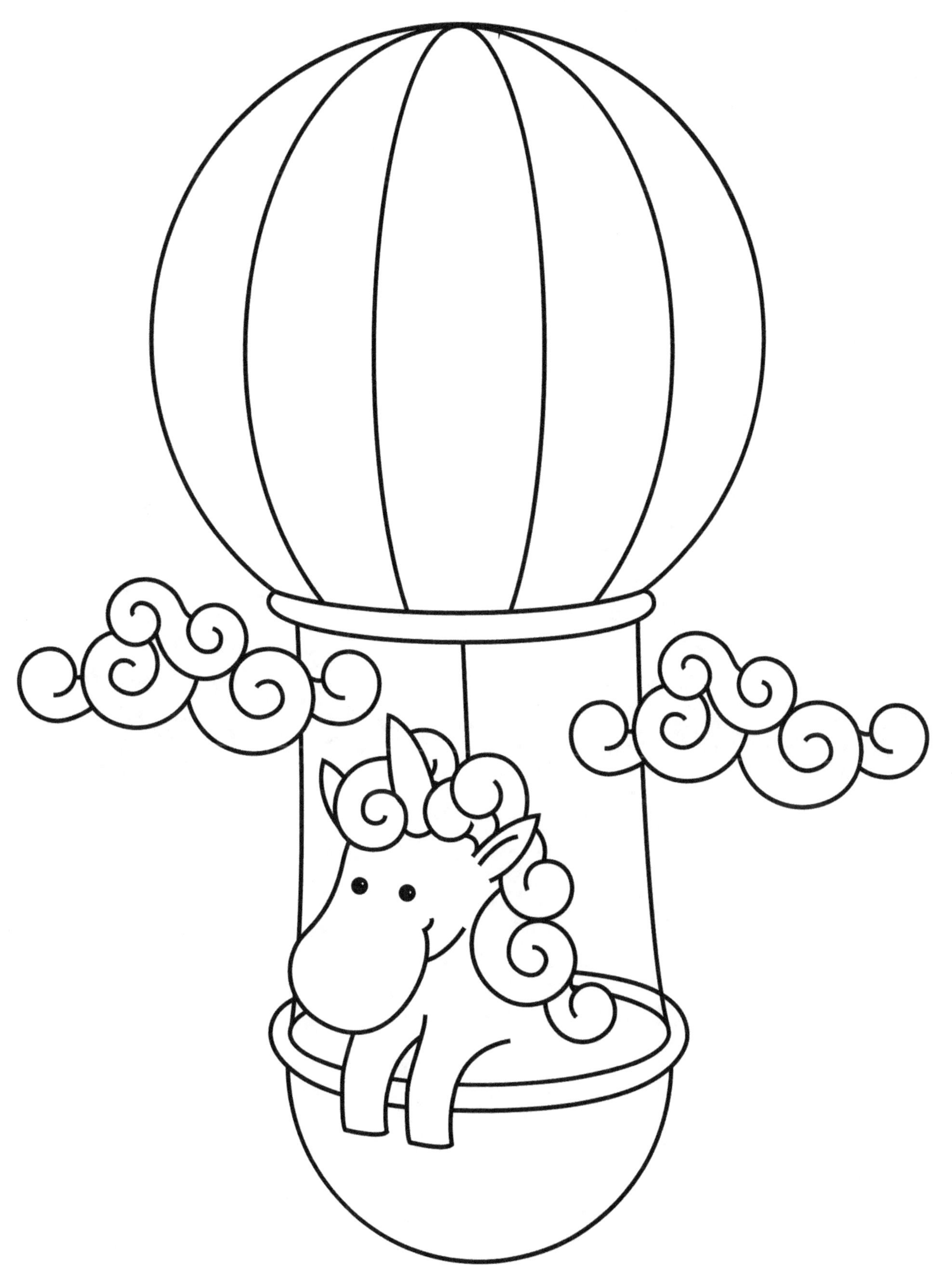

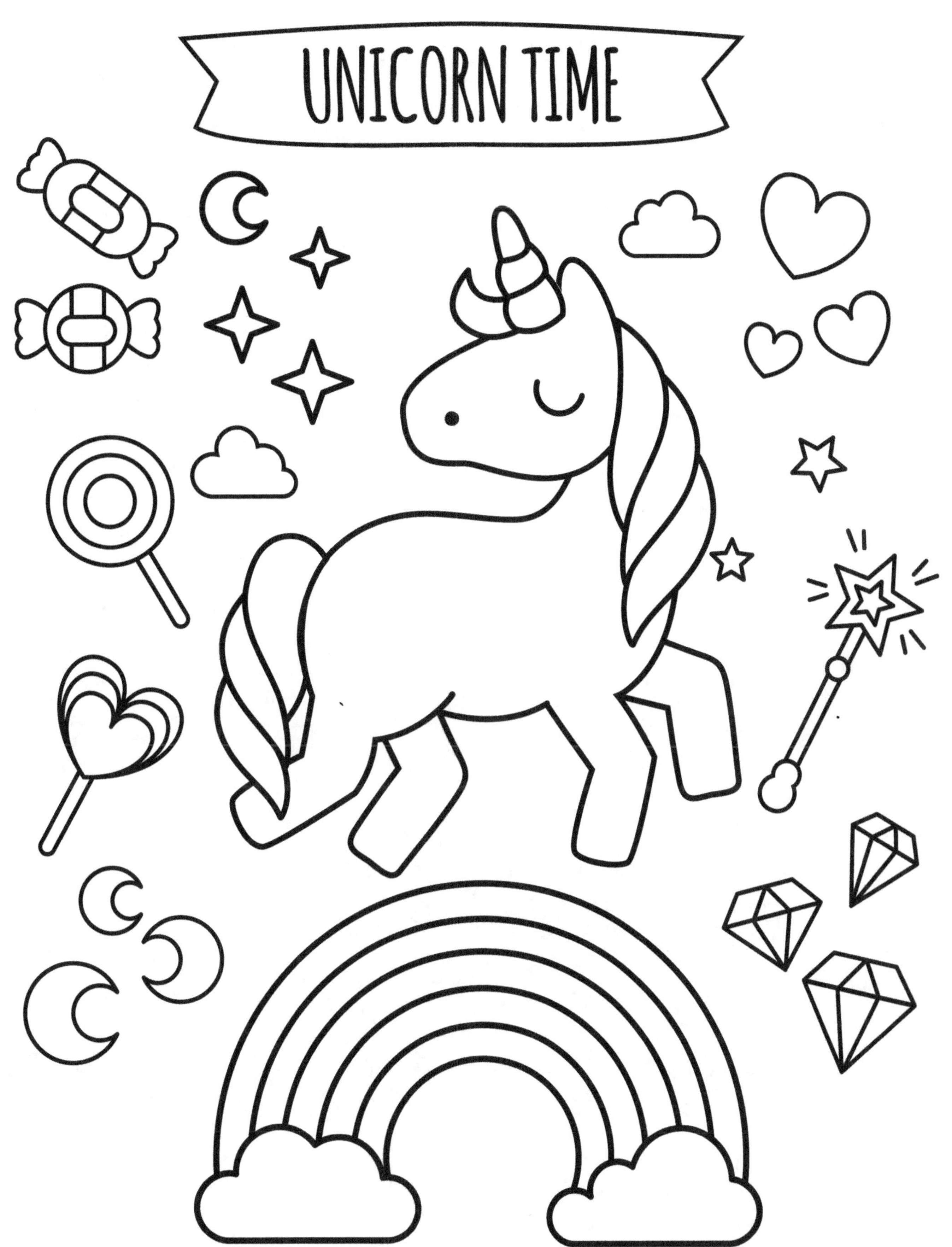
UNICORN TIME

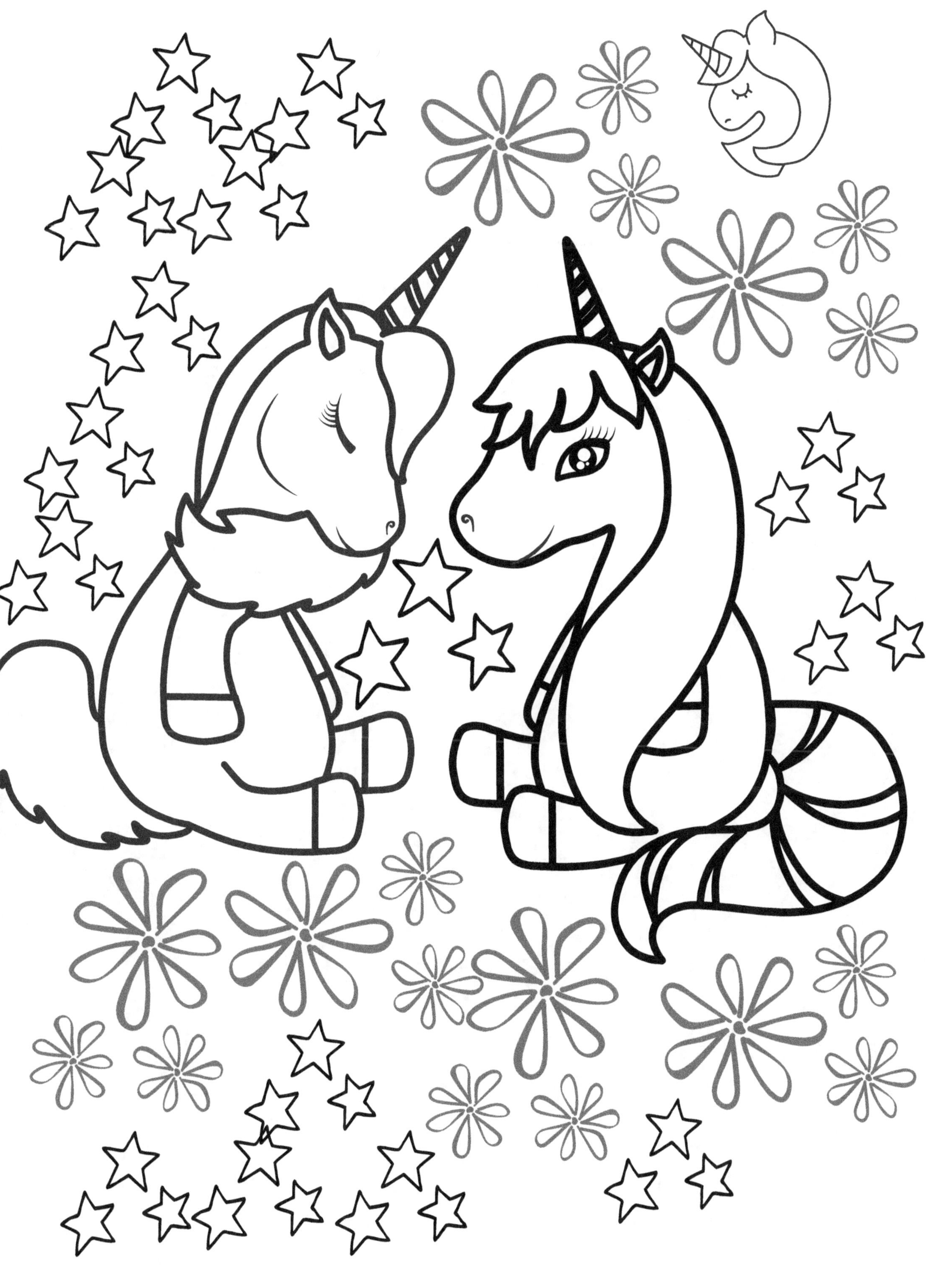

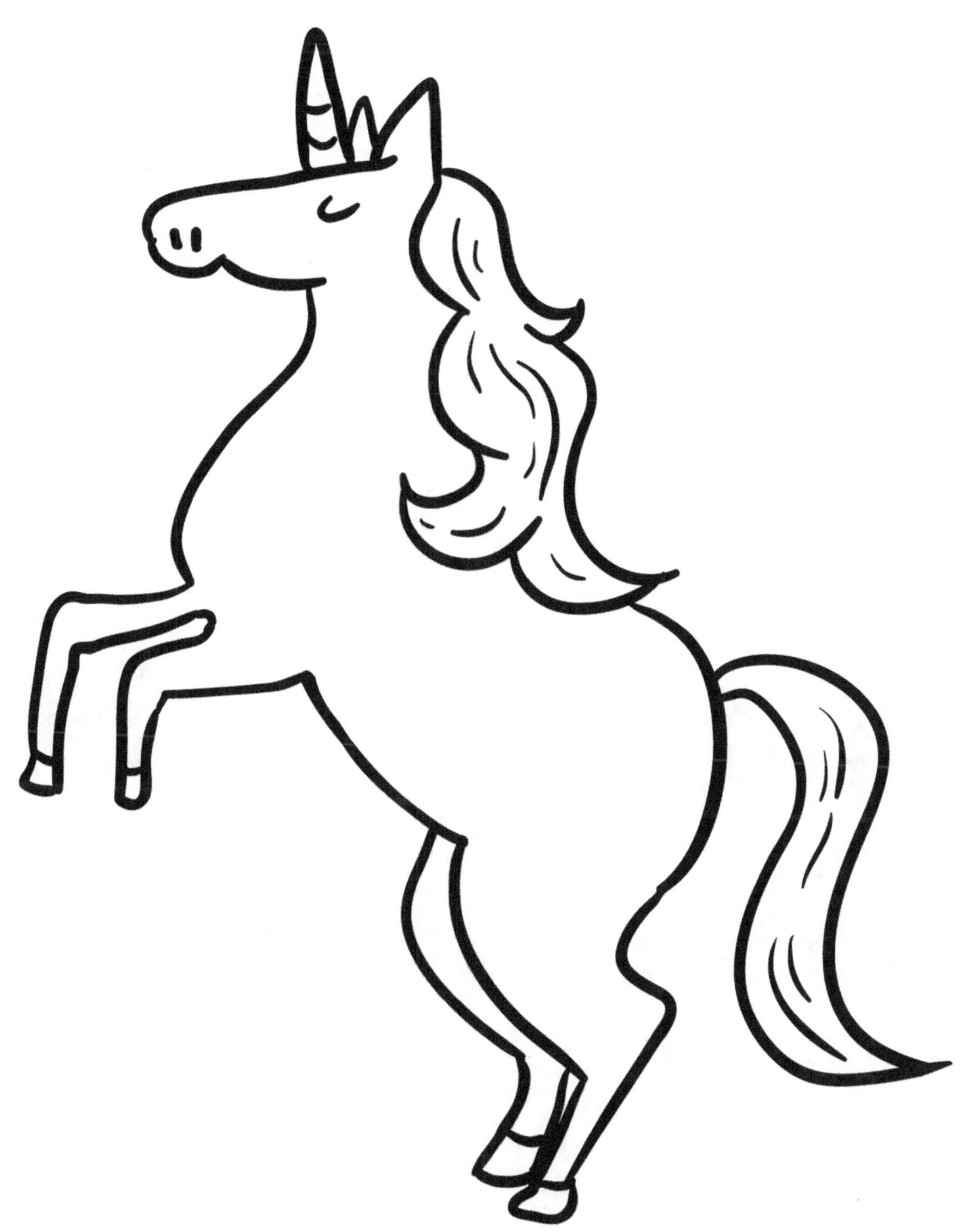

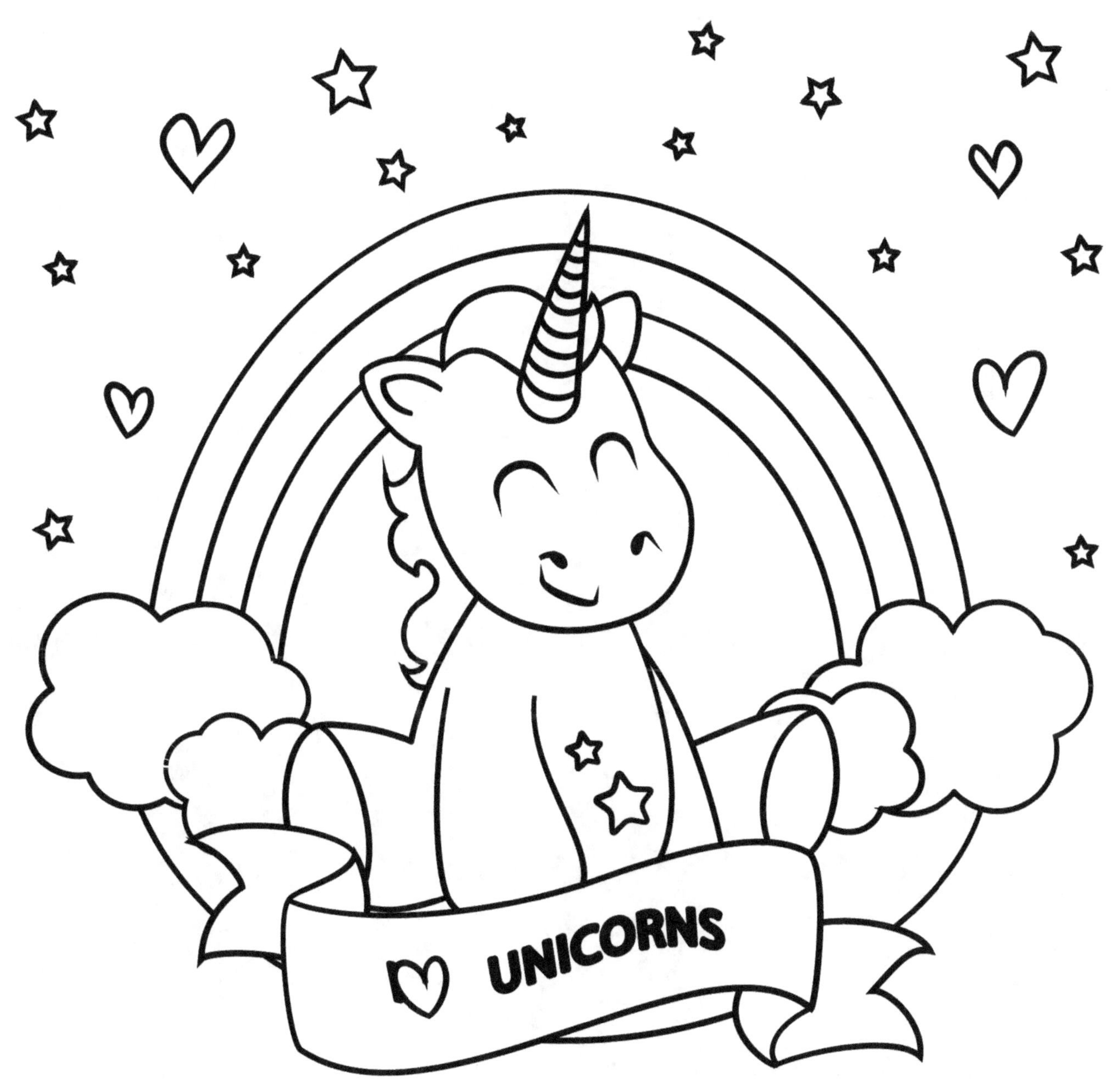
UNICORNS

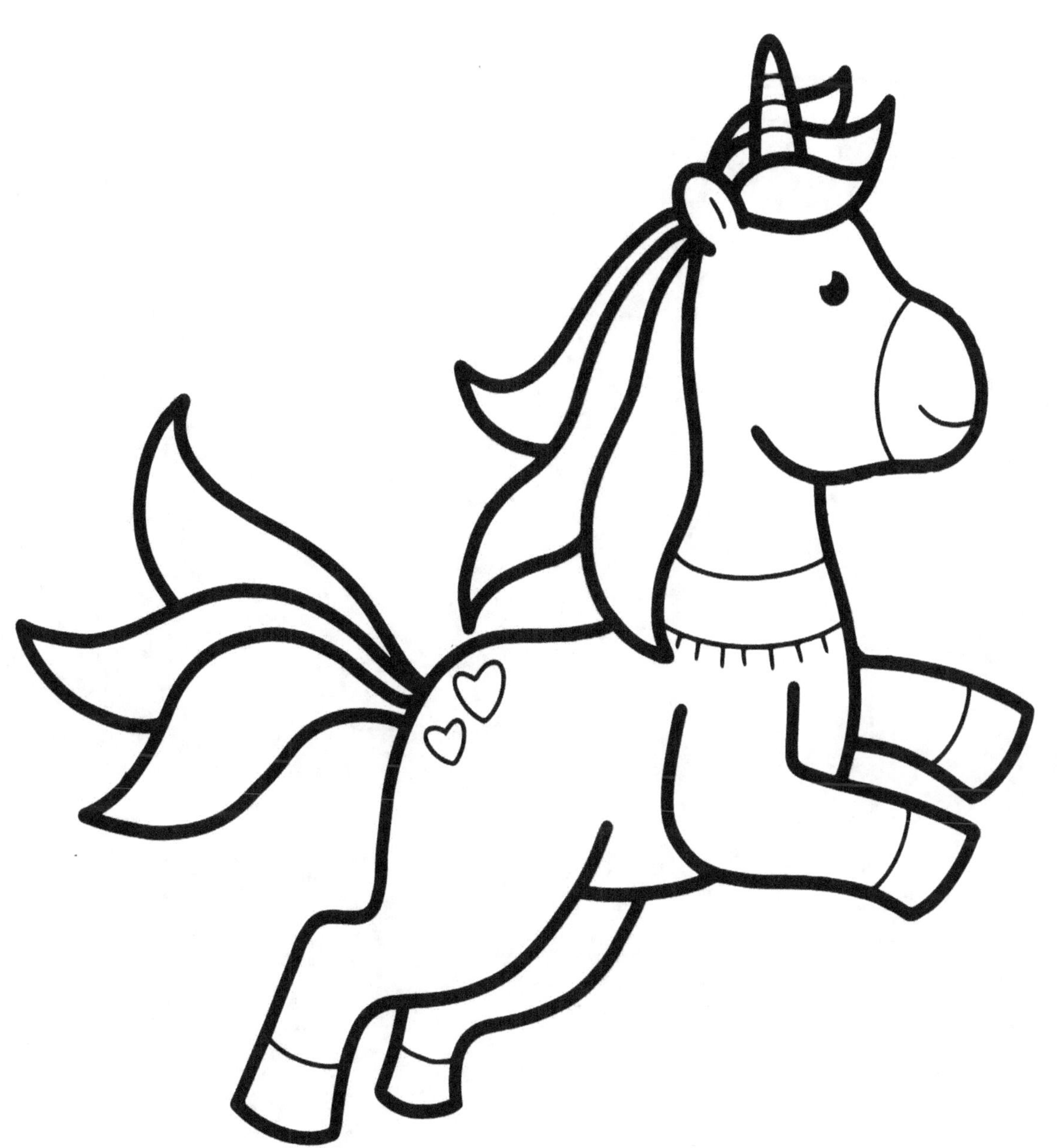

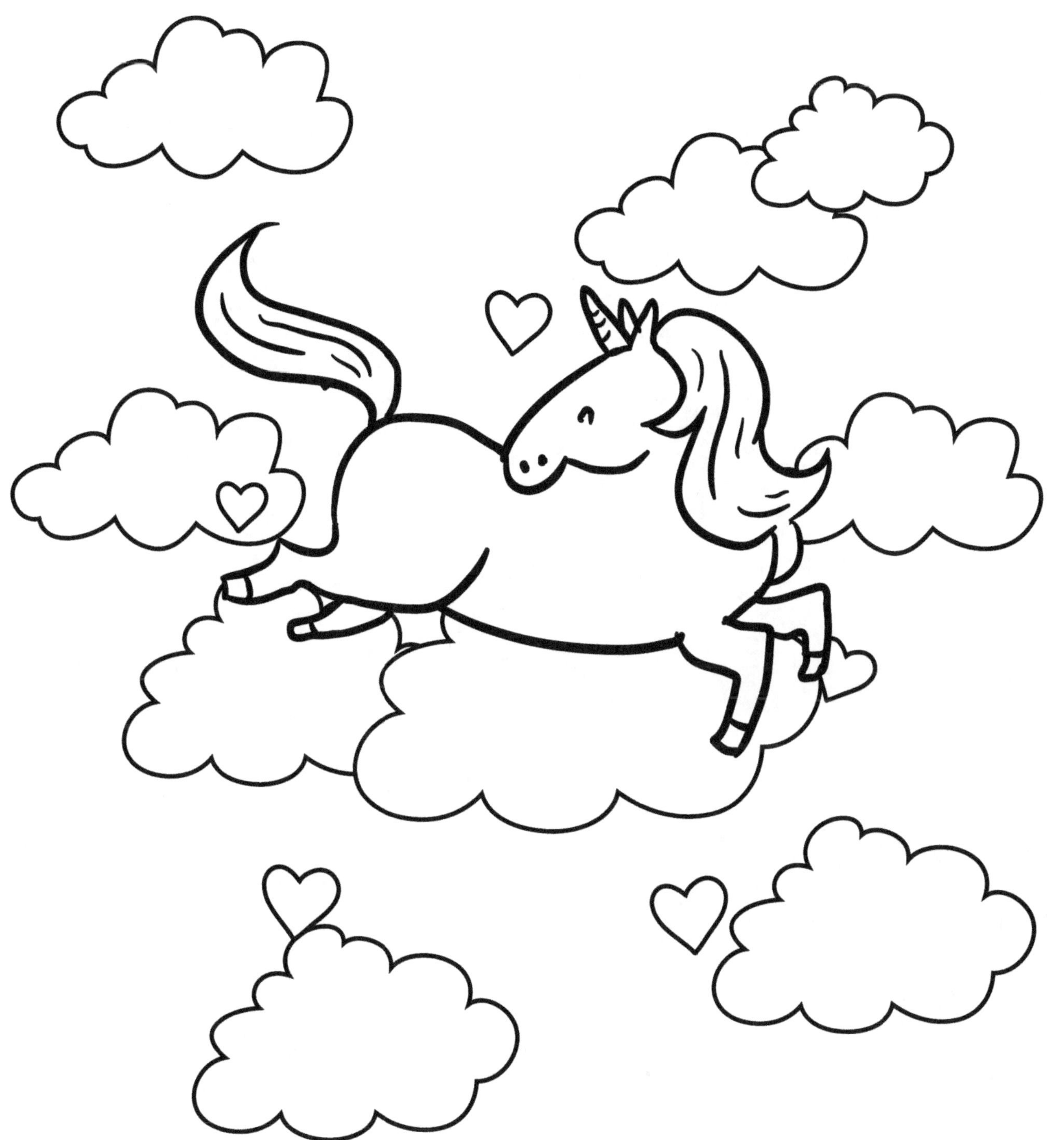

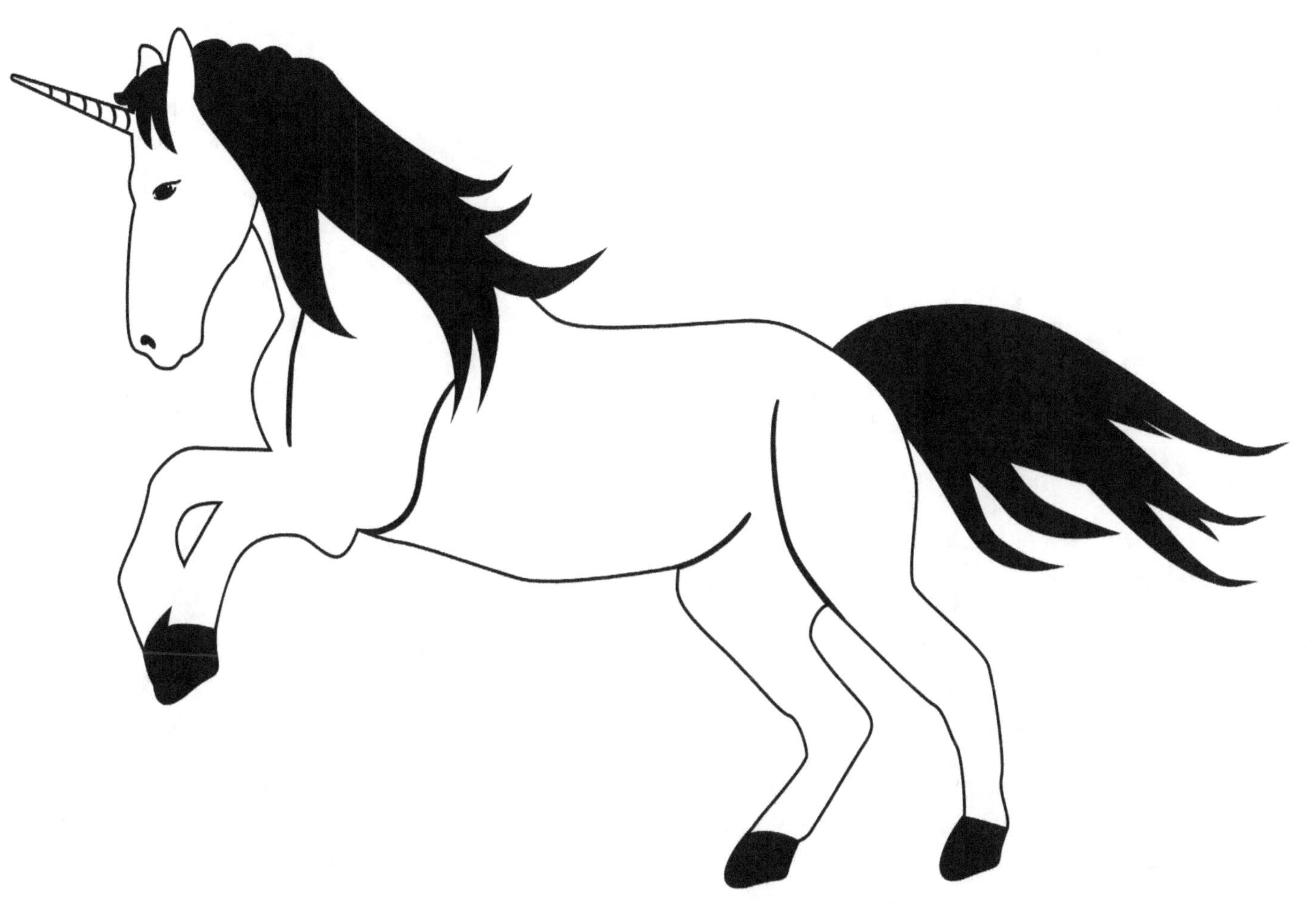

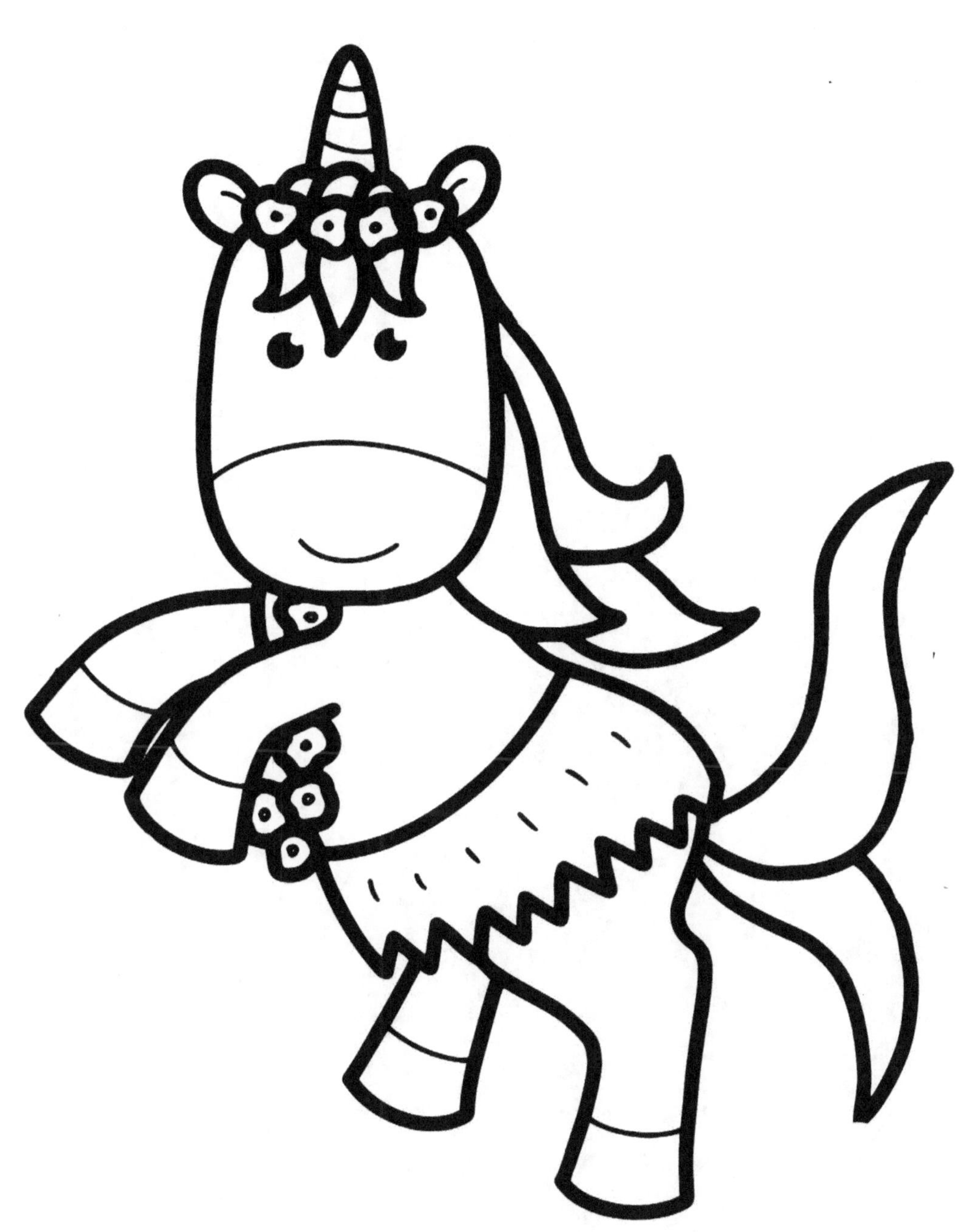

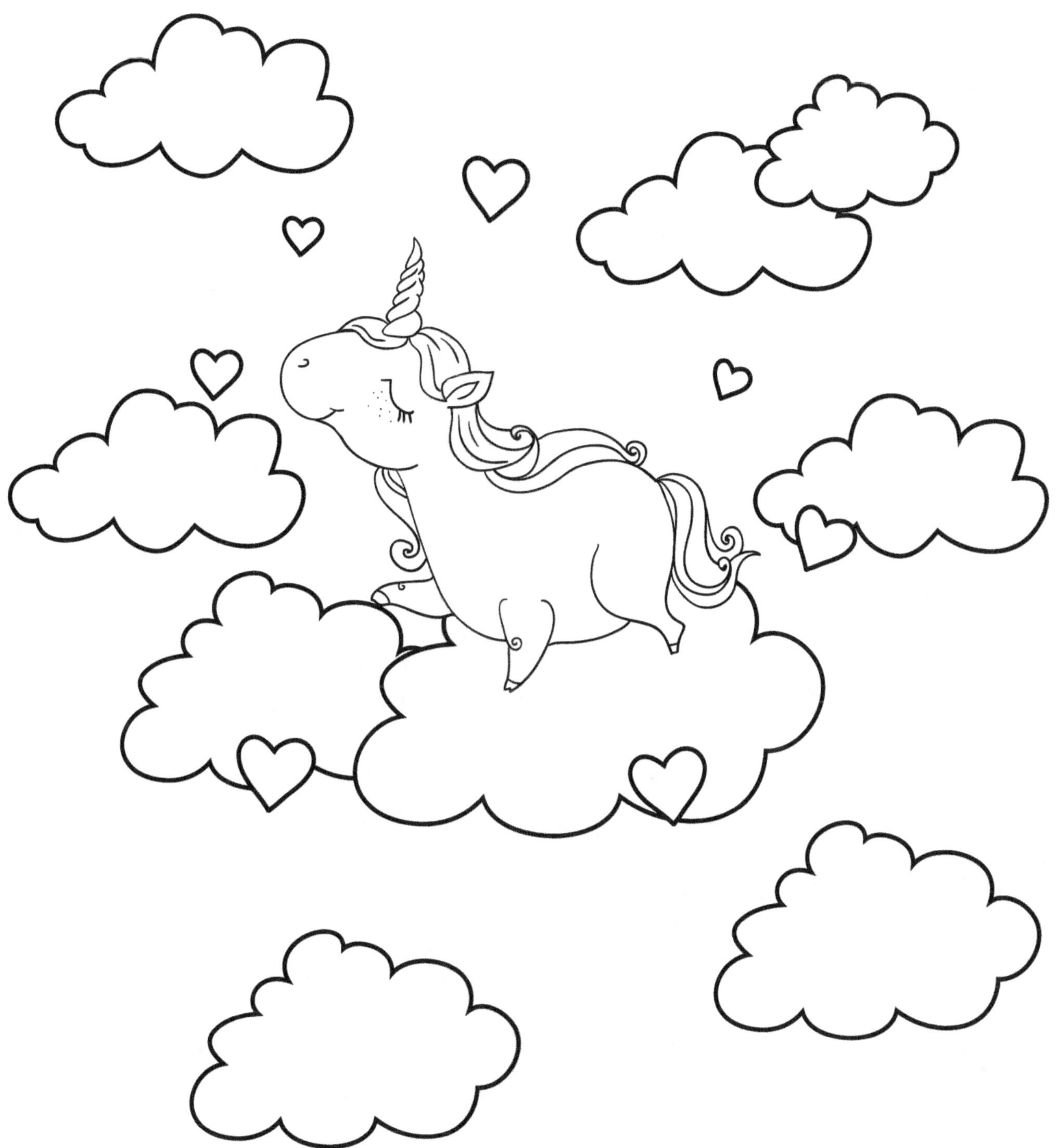

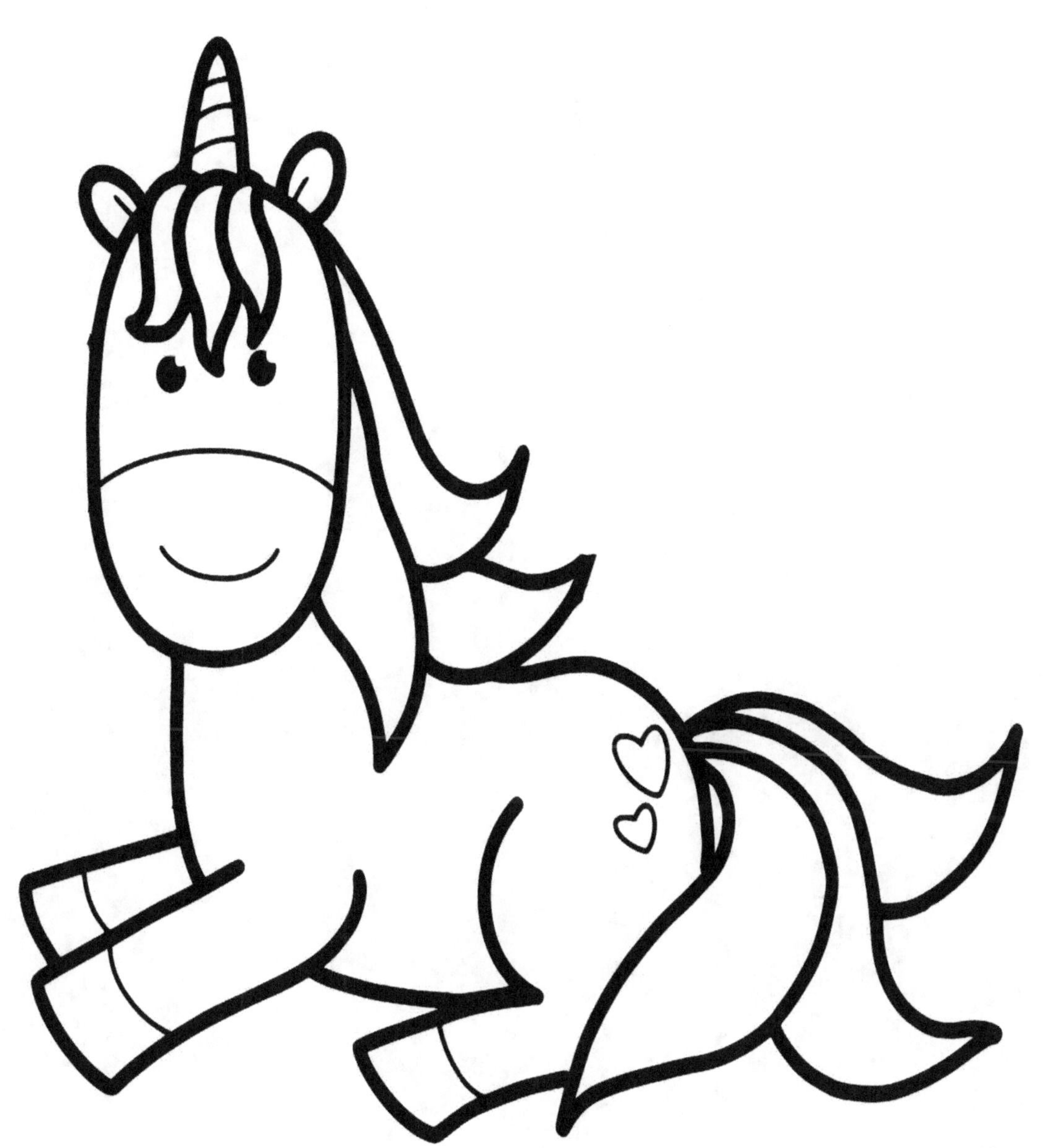

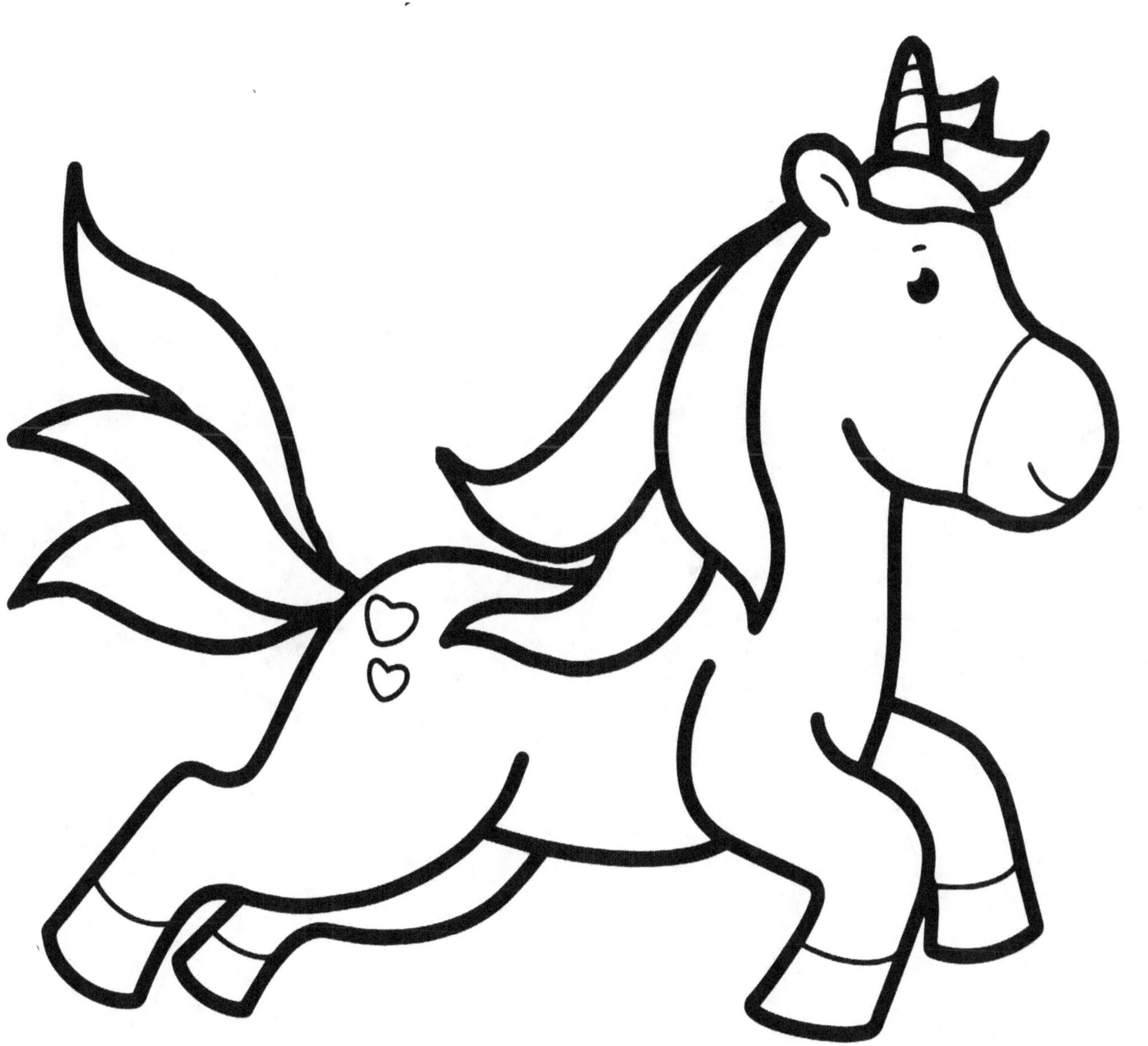

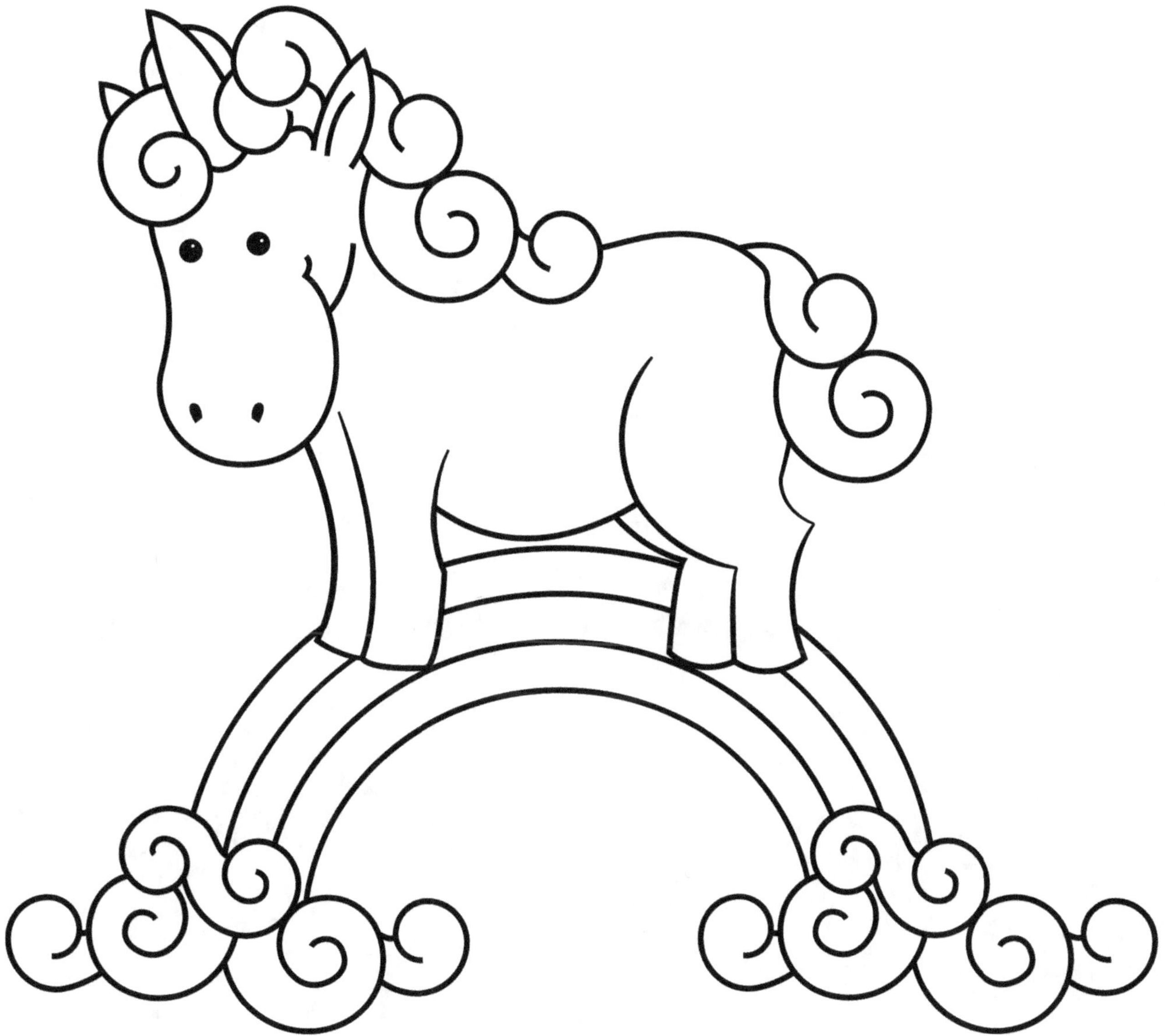

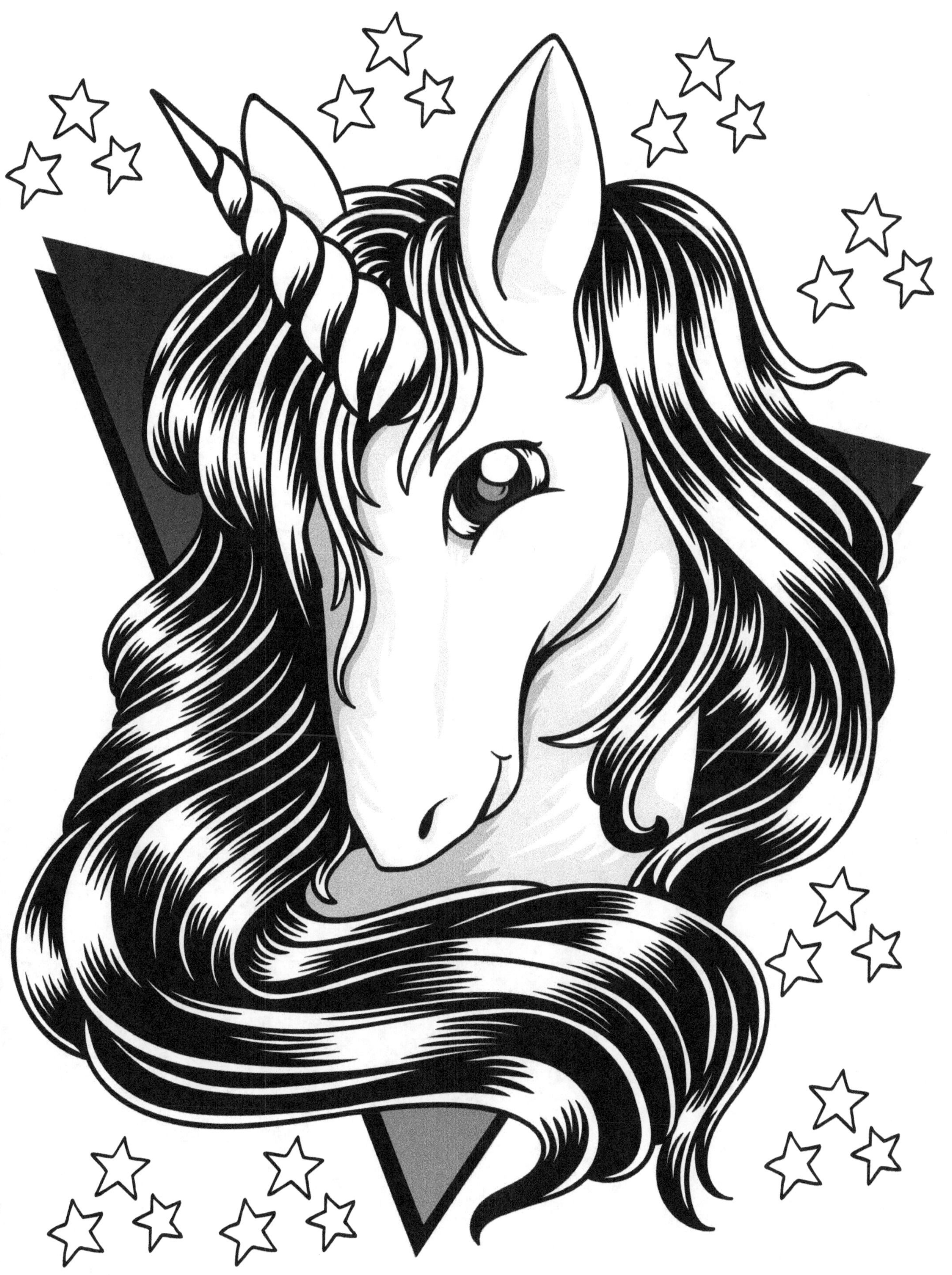

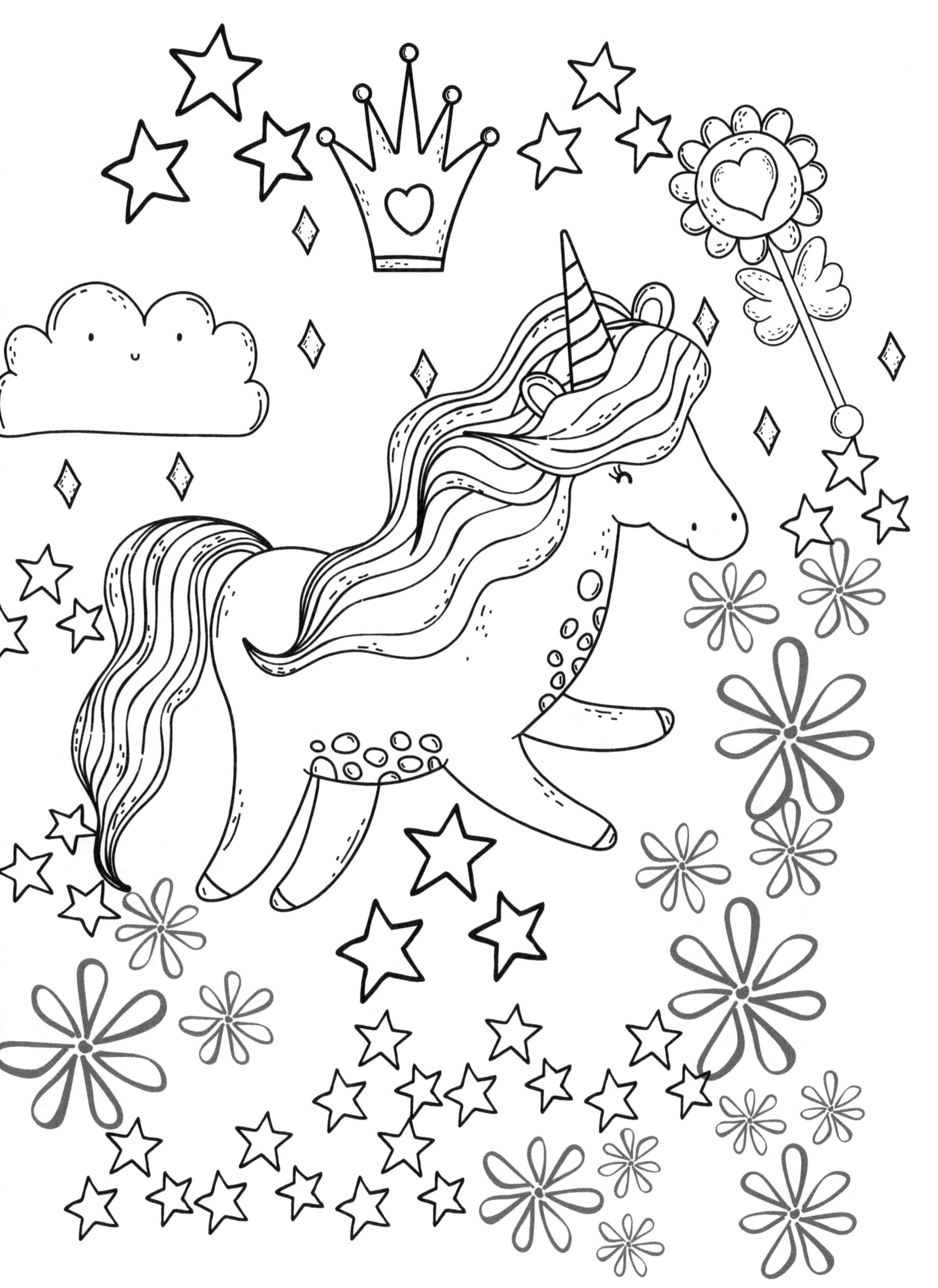

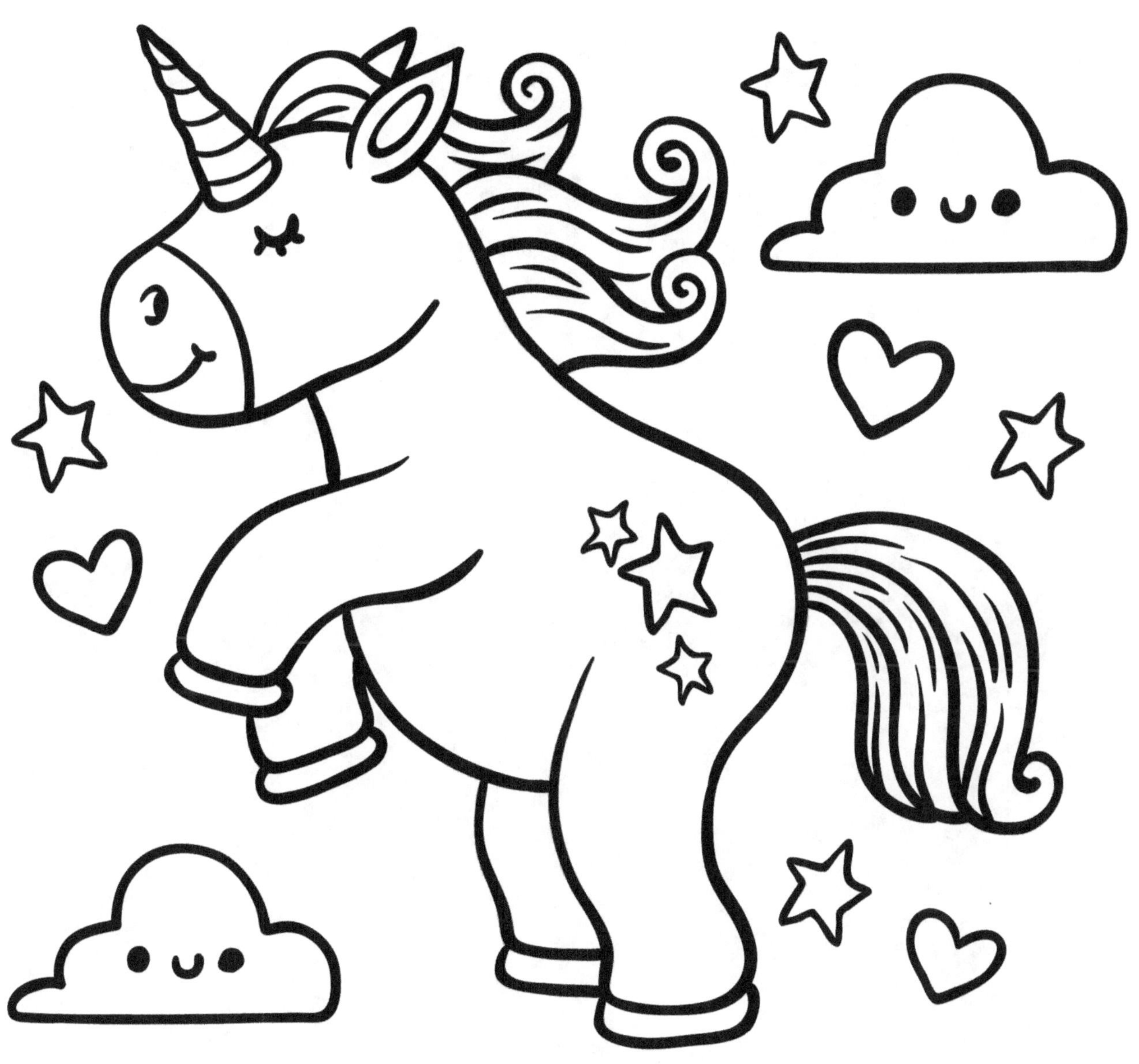

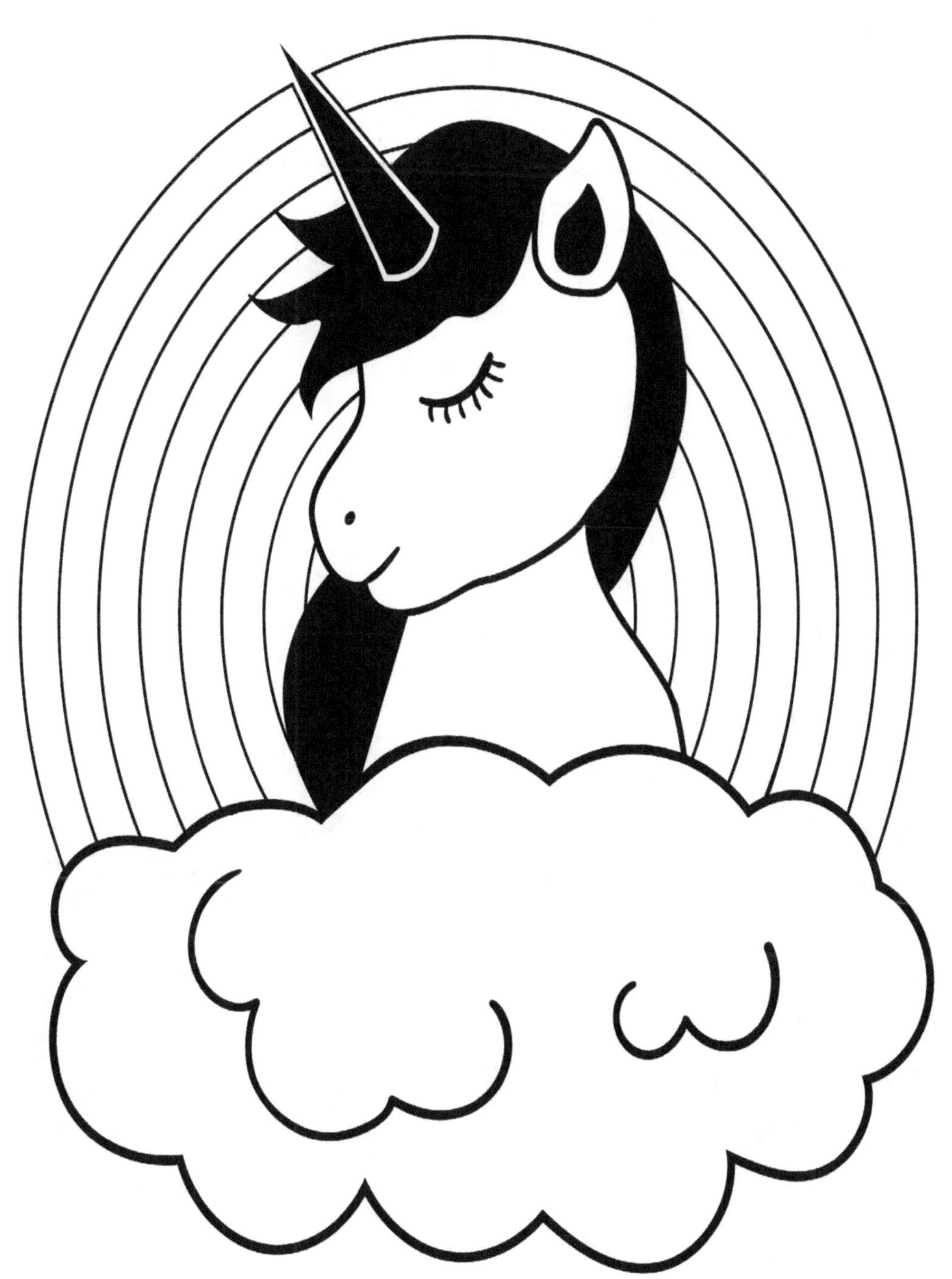

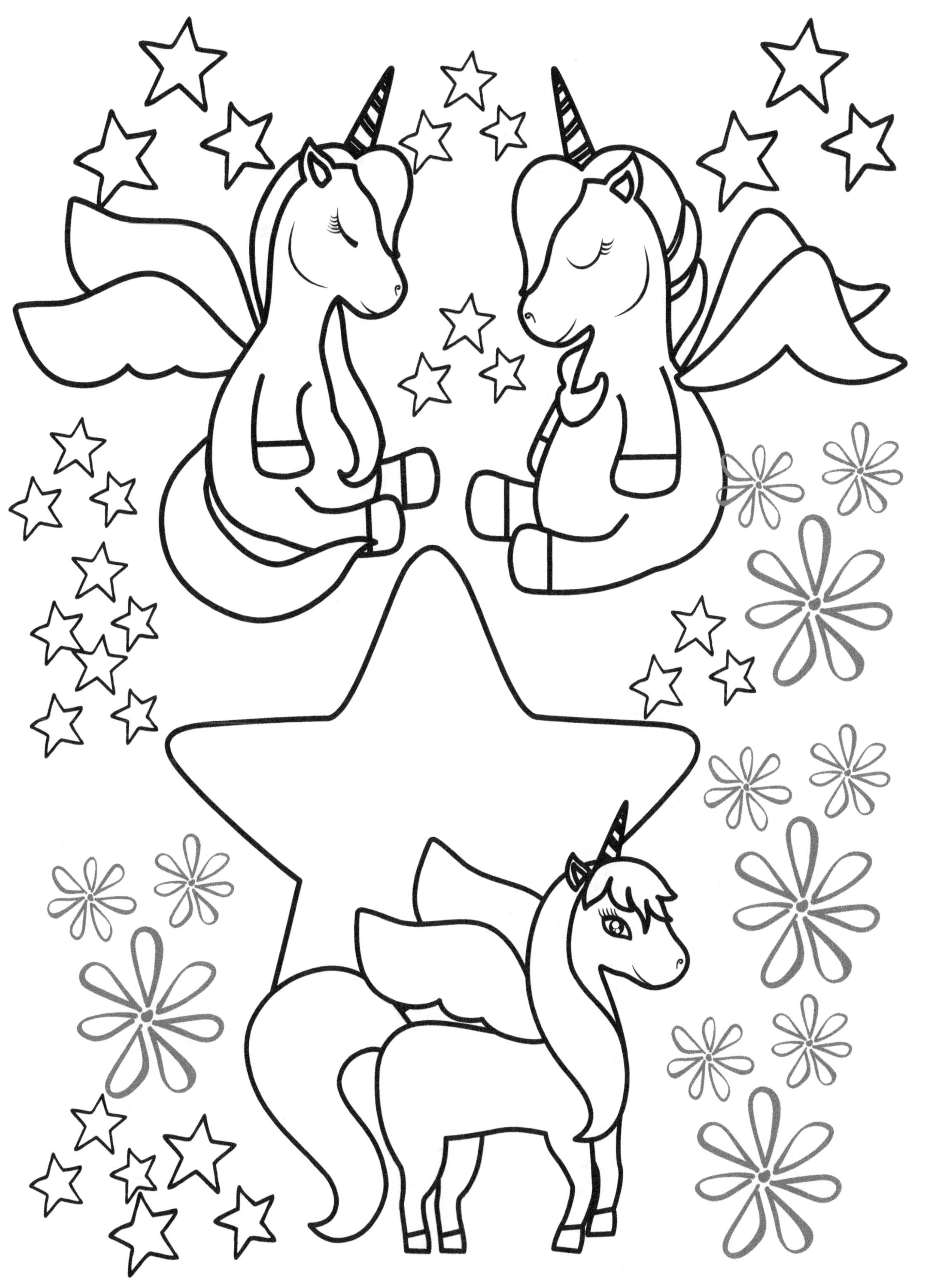

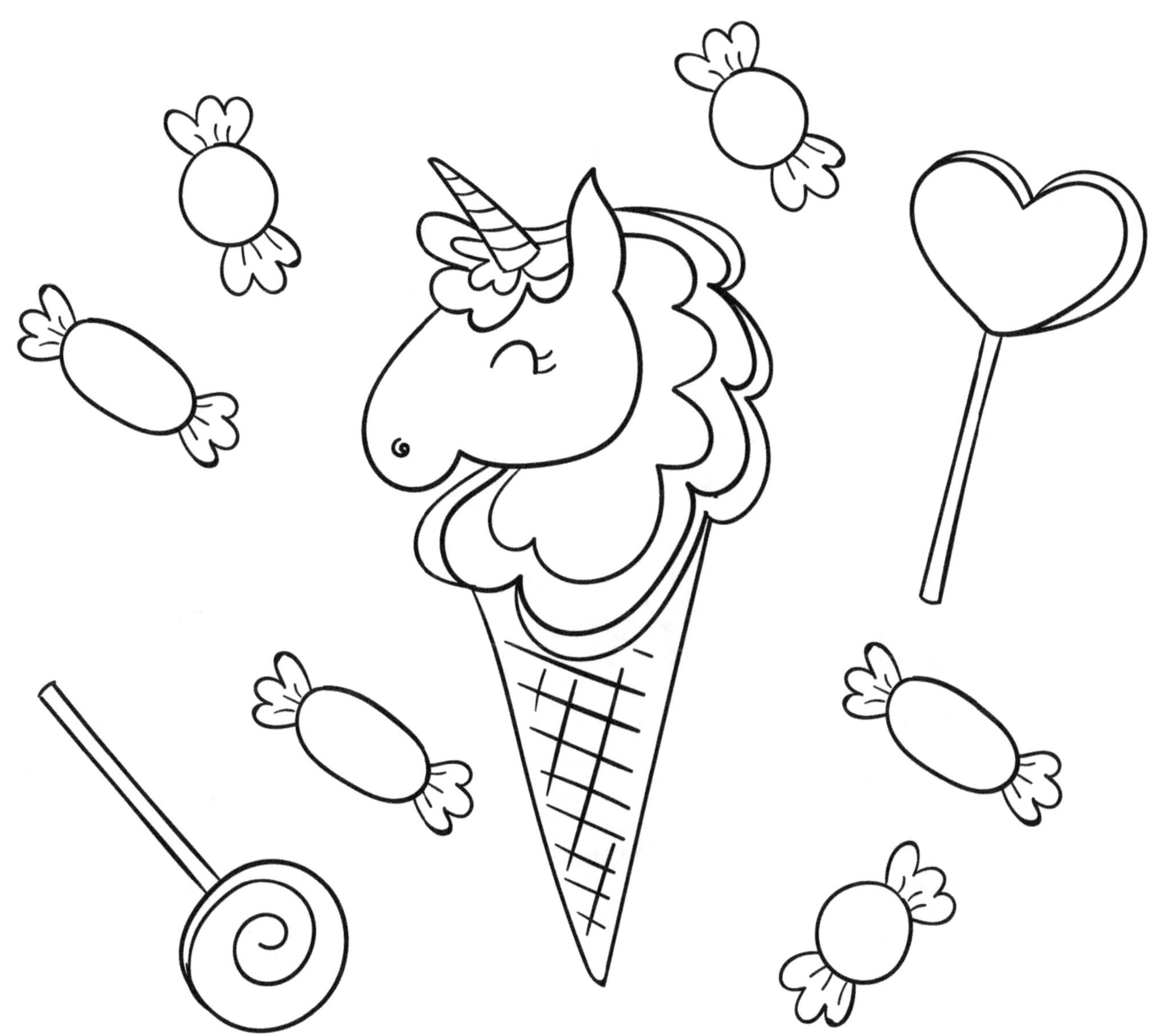

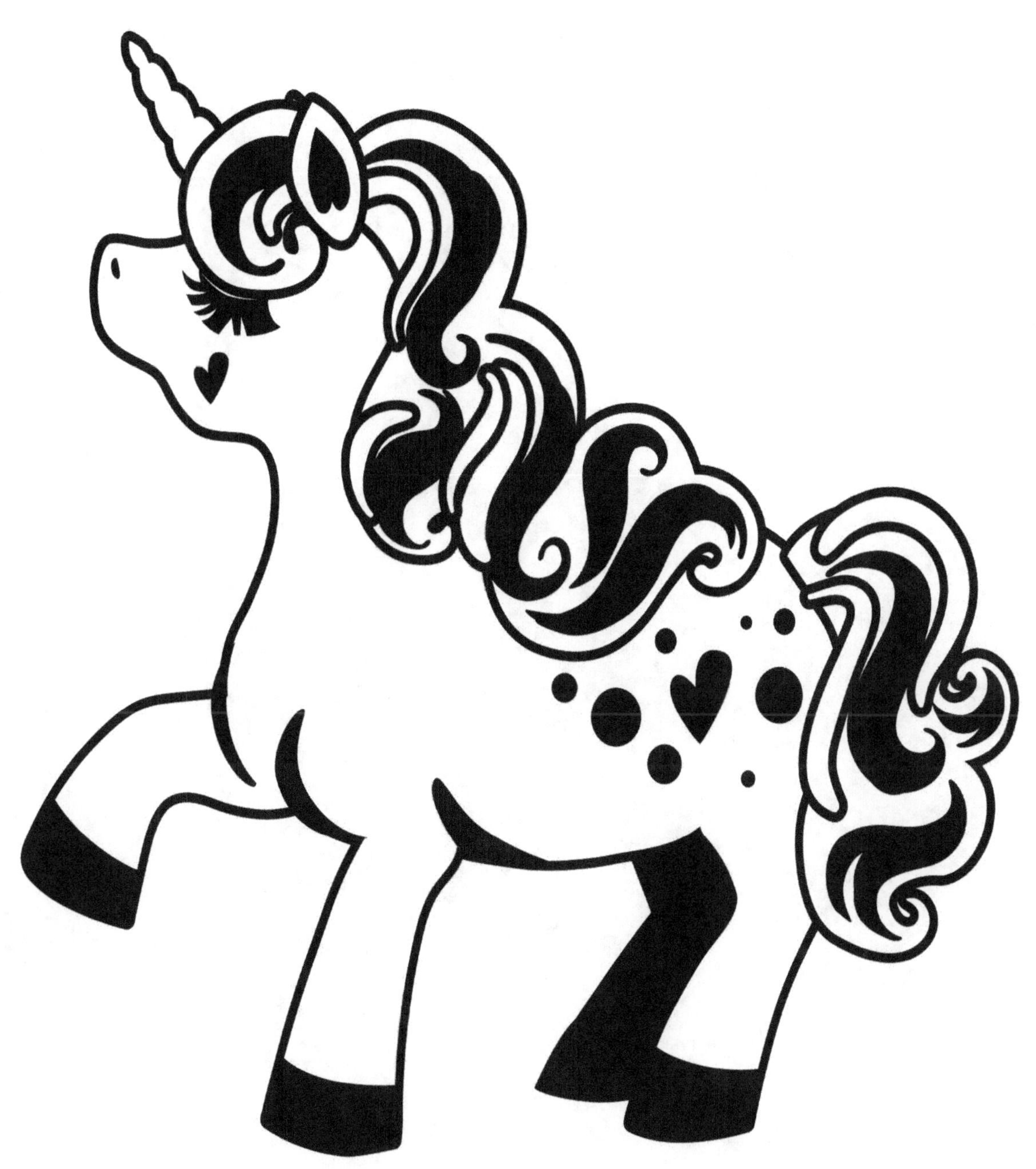

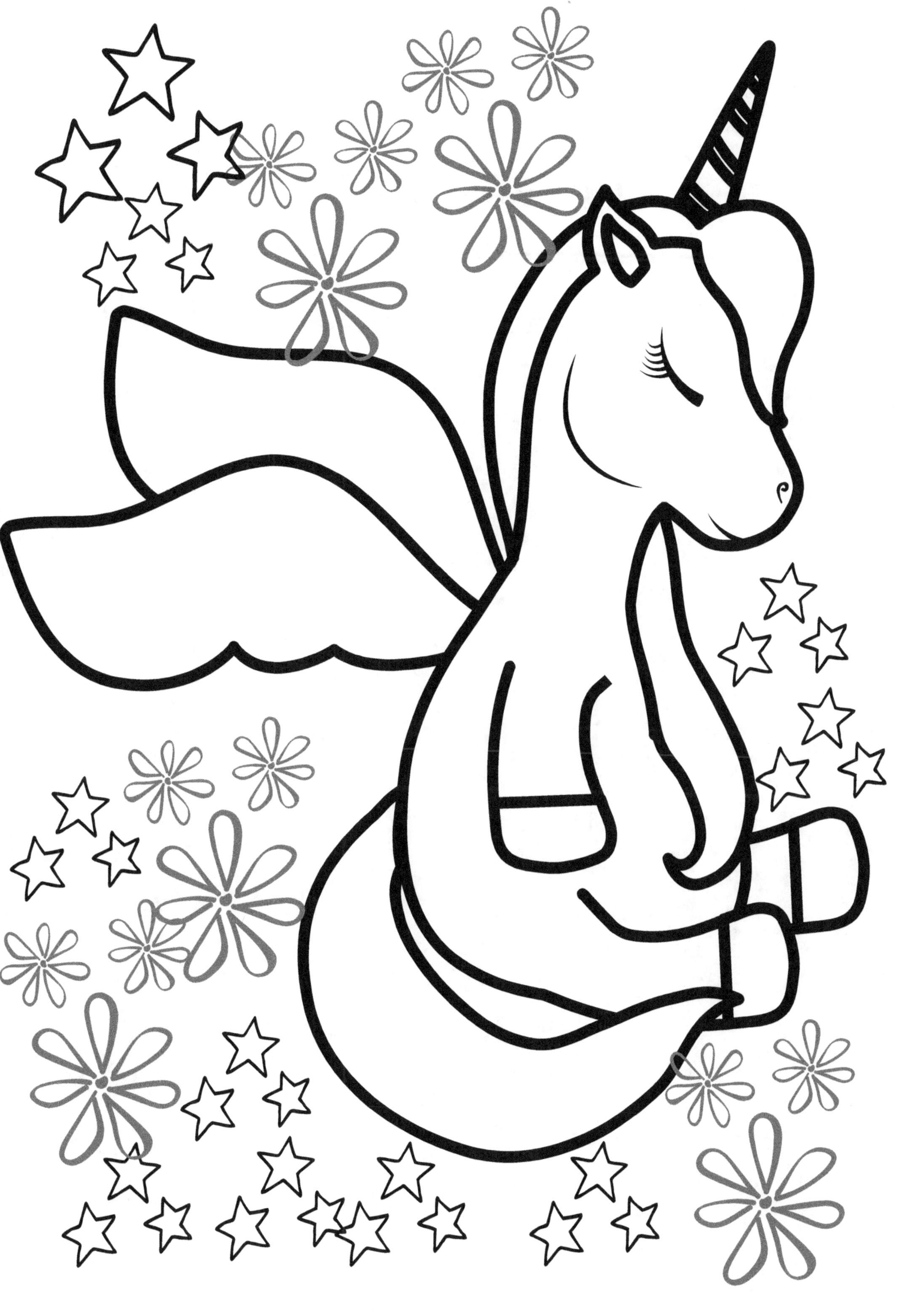

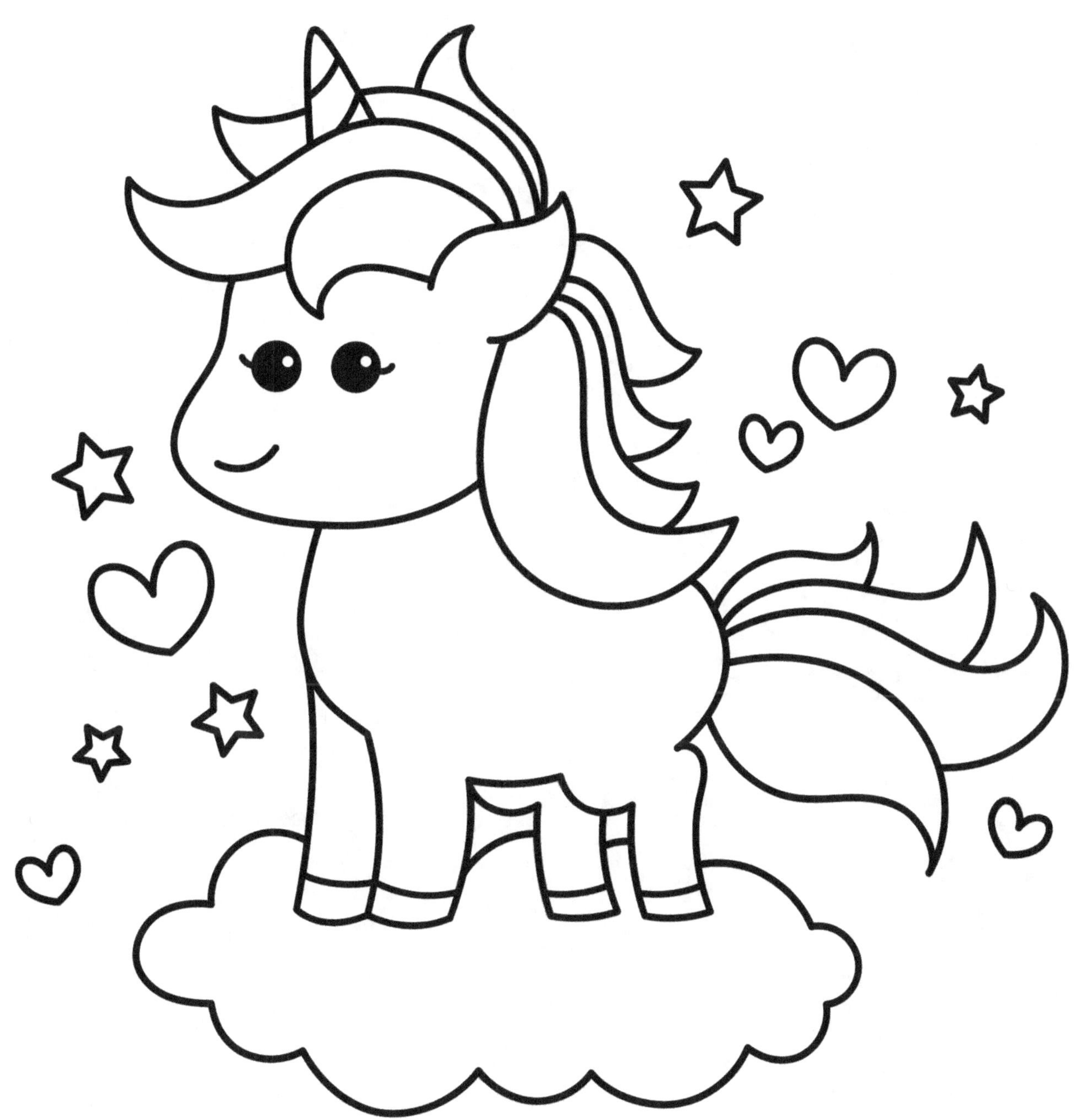

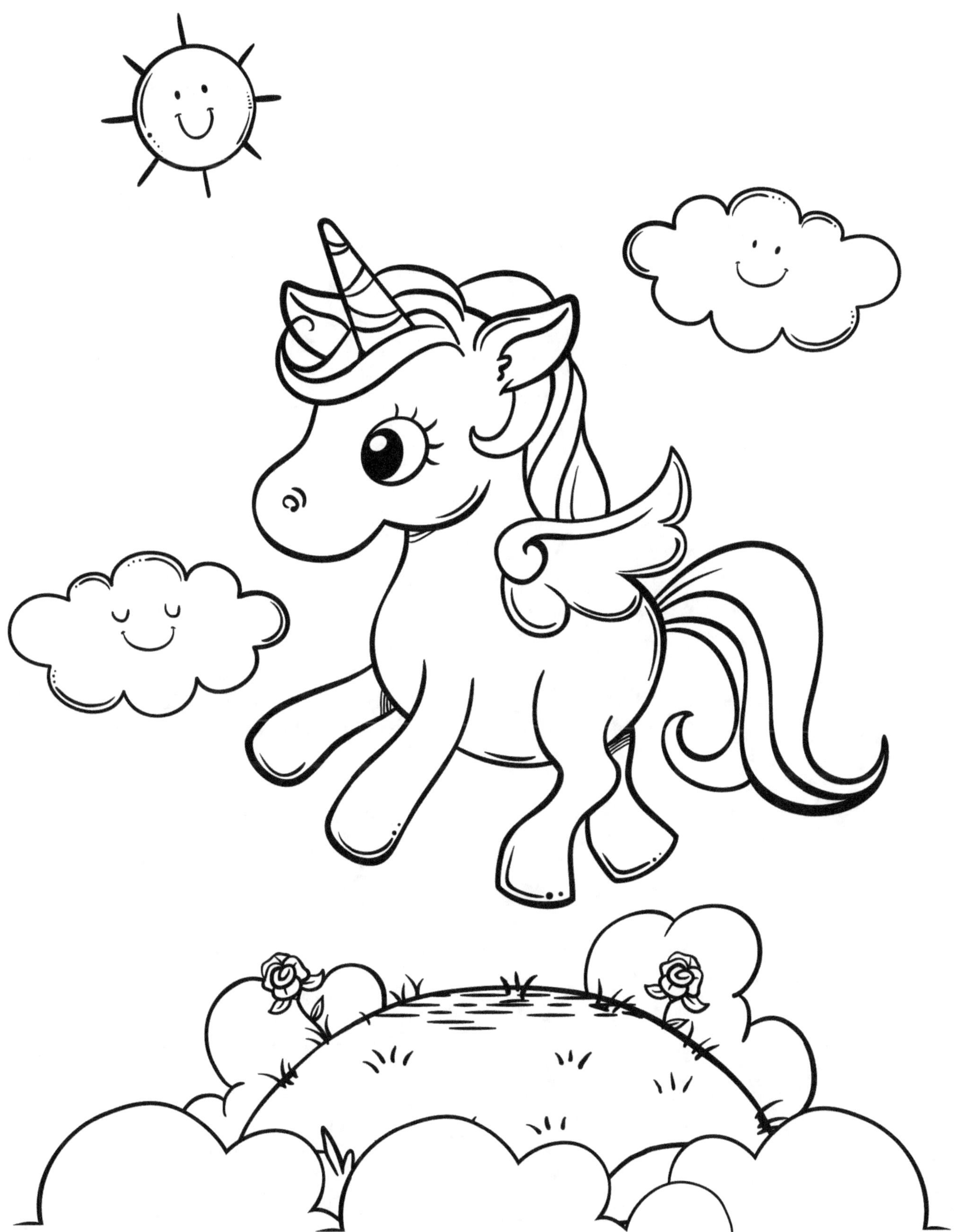

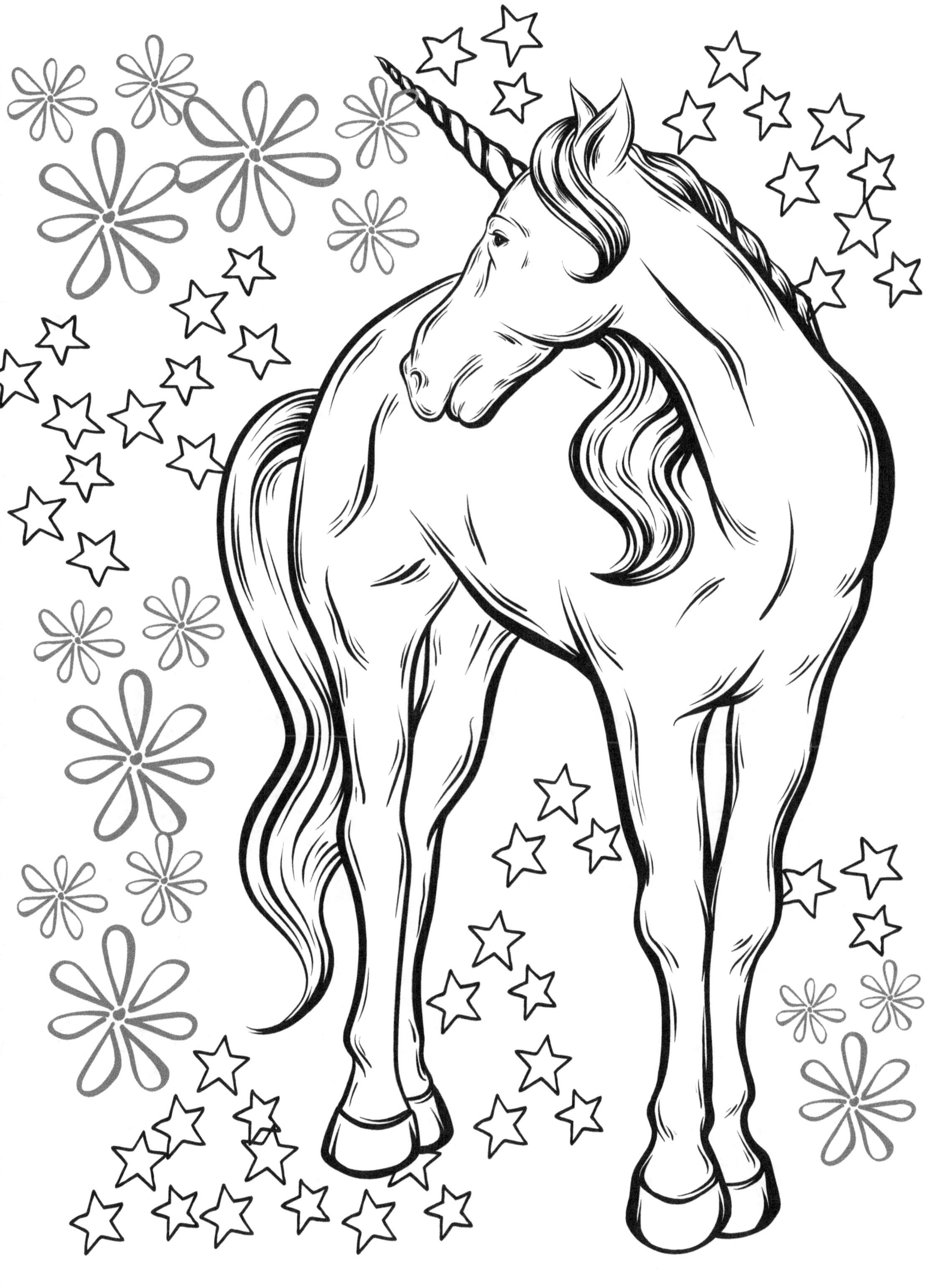

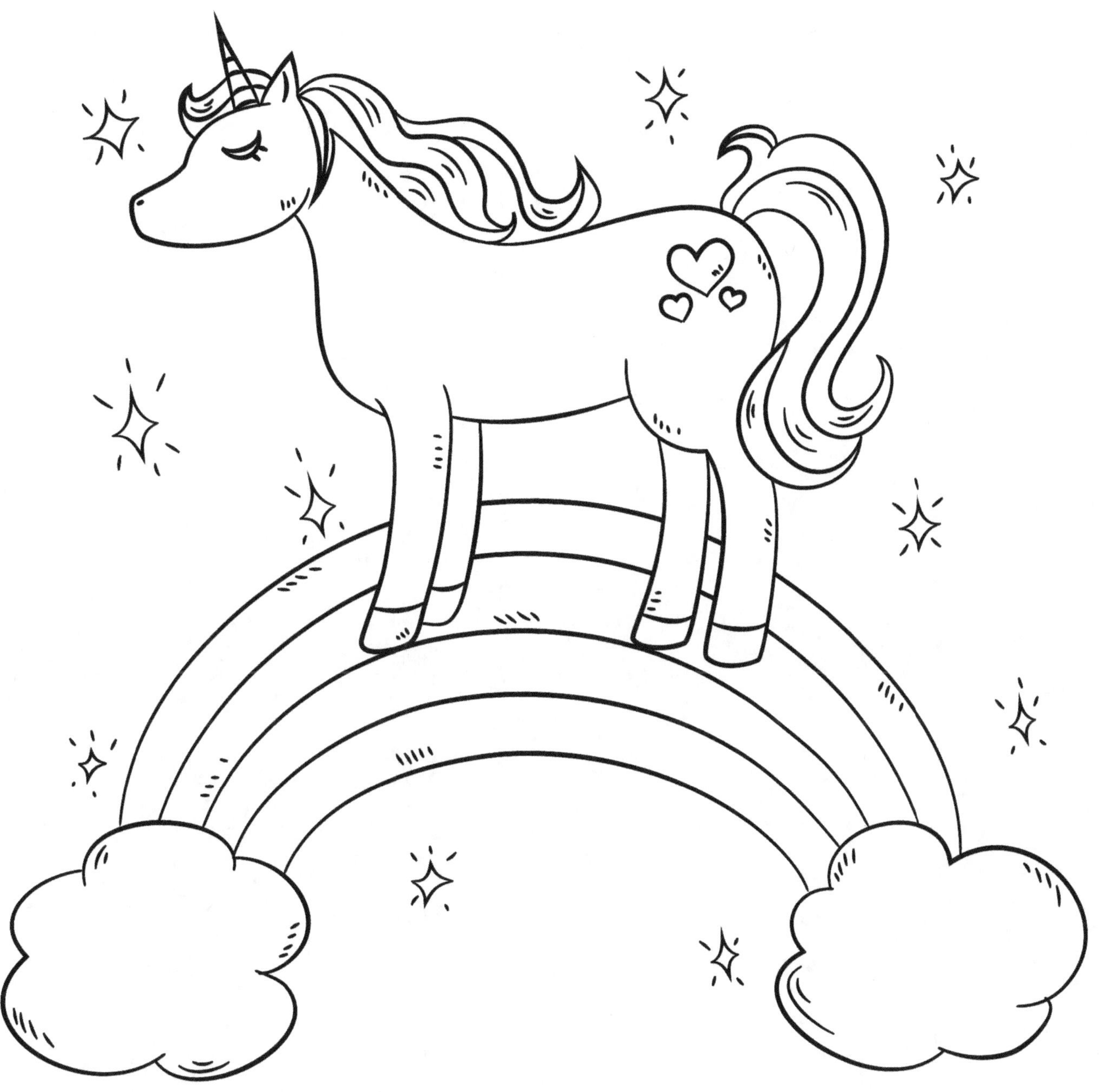

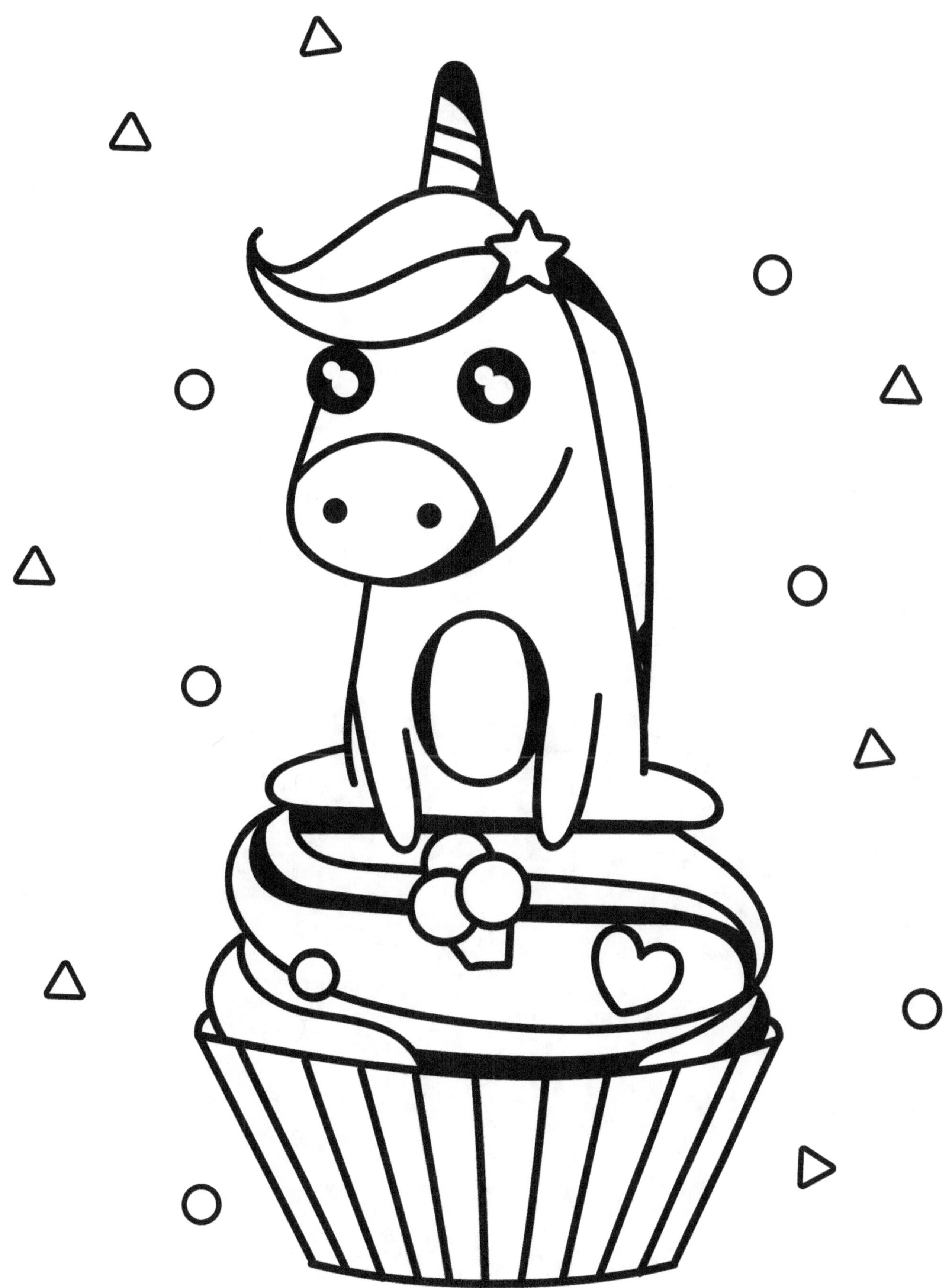

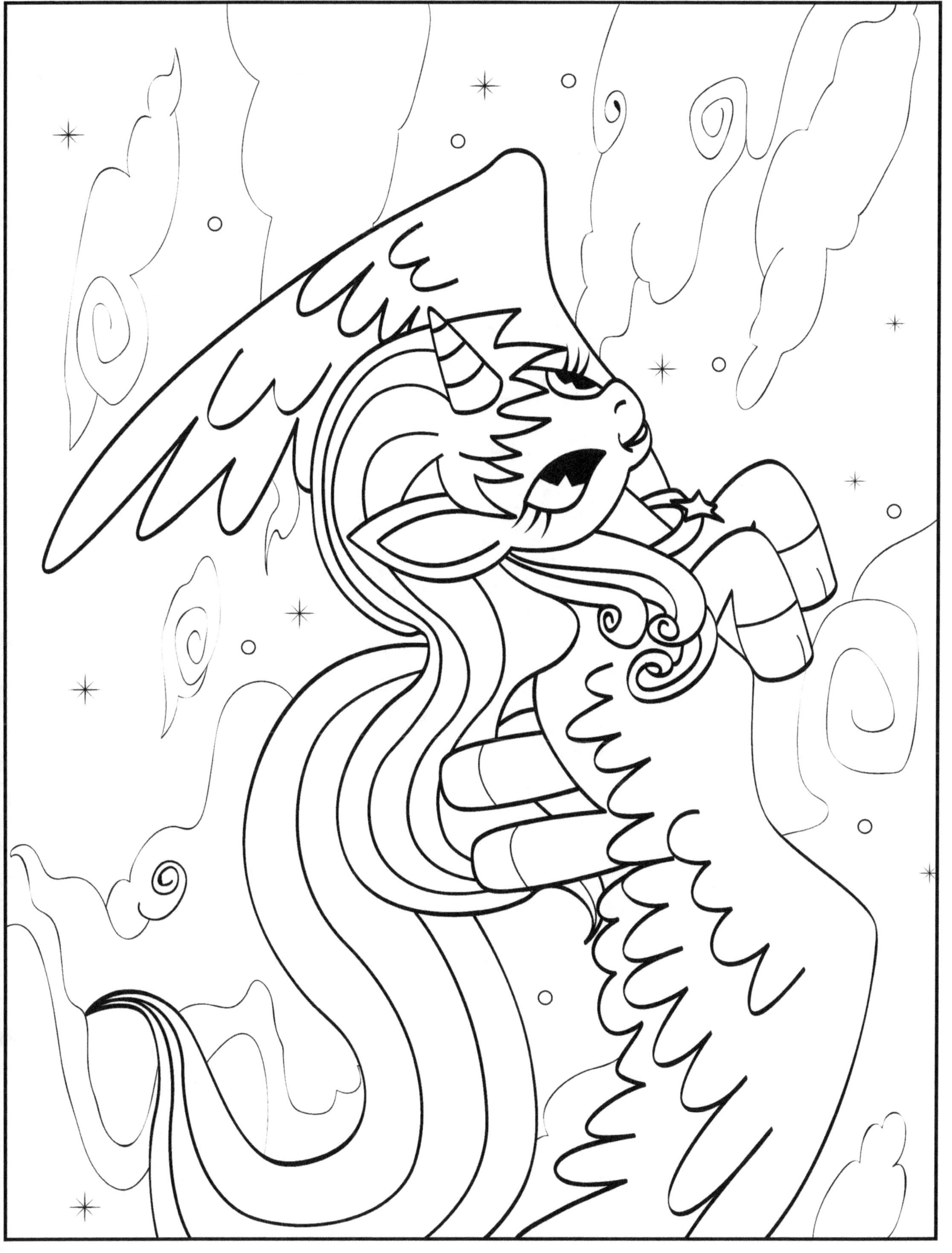

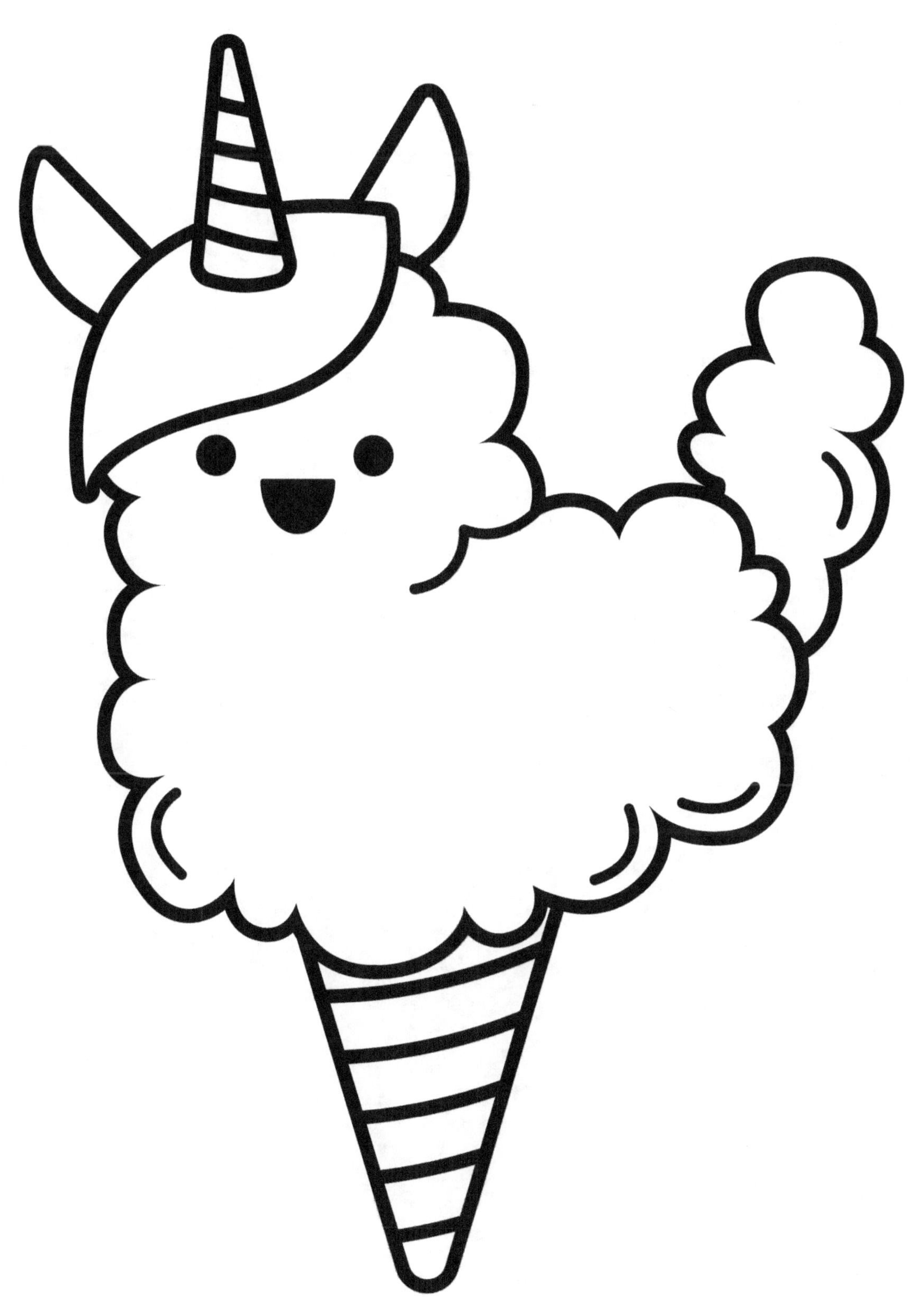

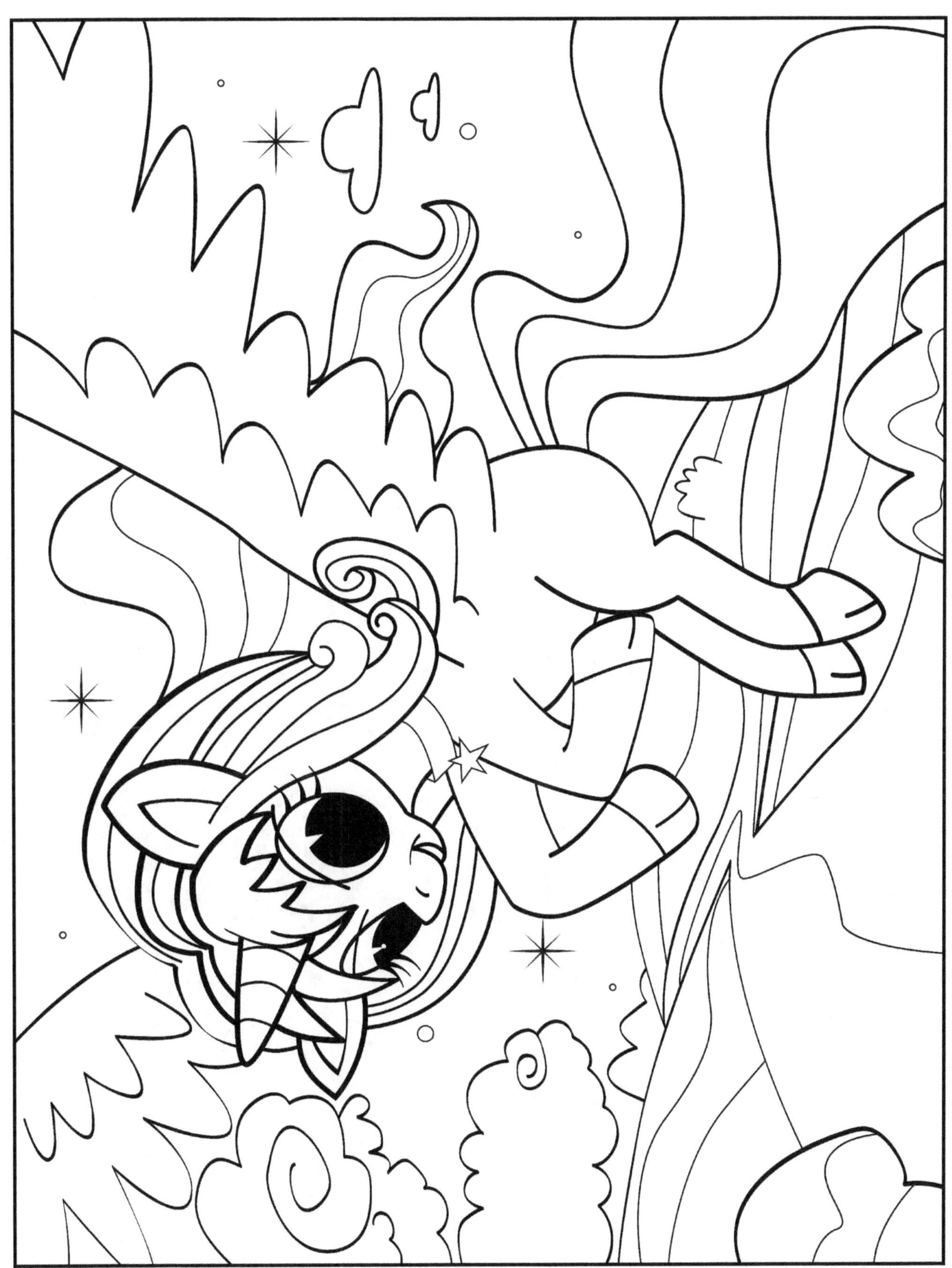

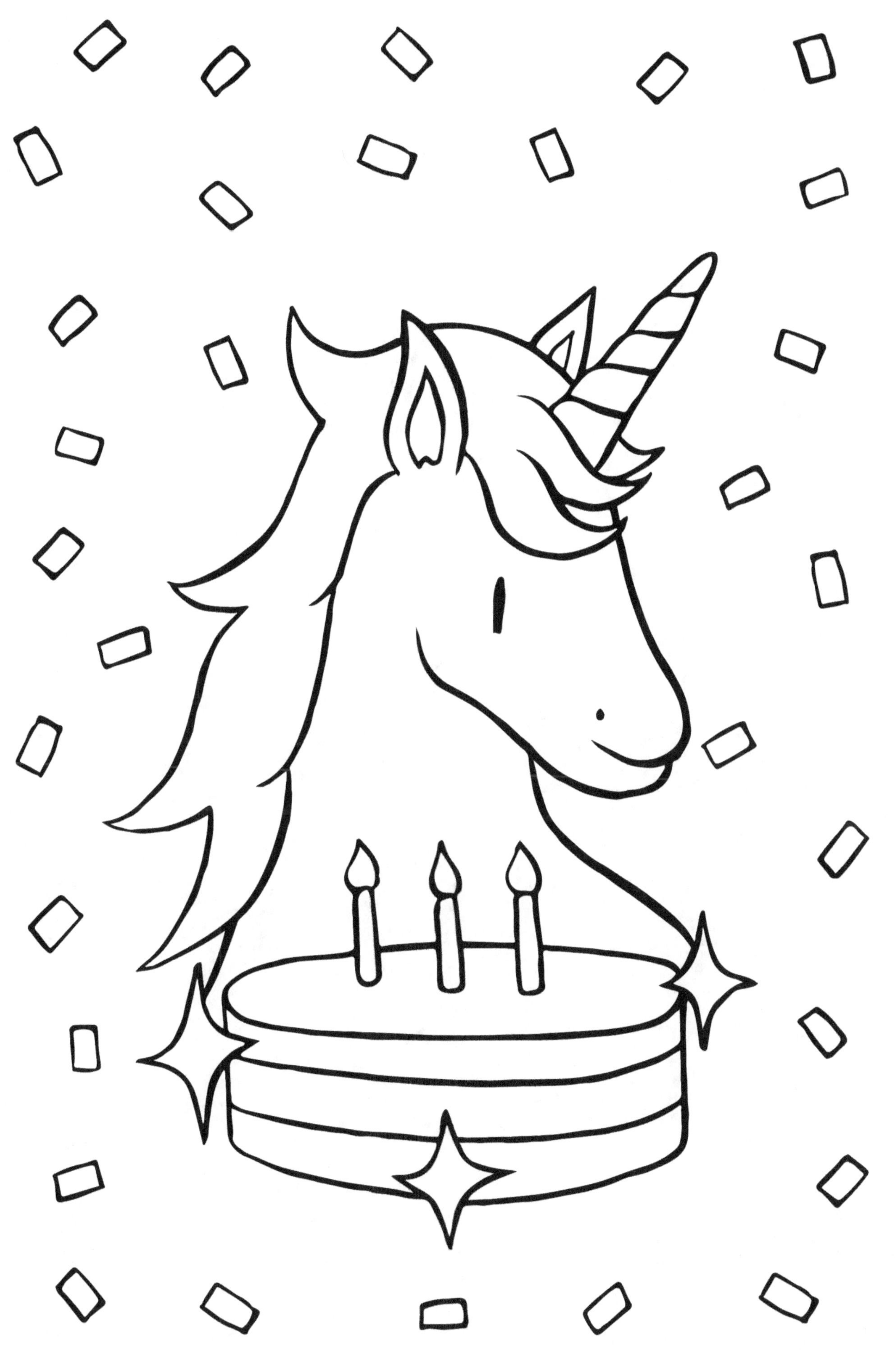

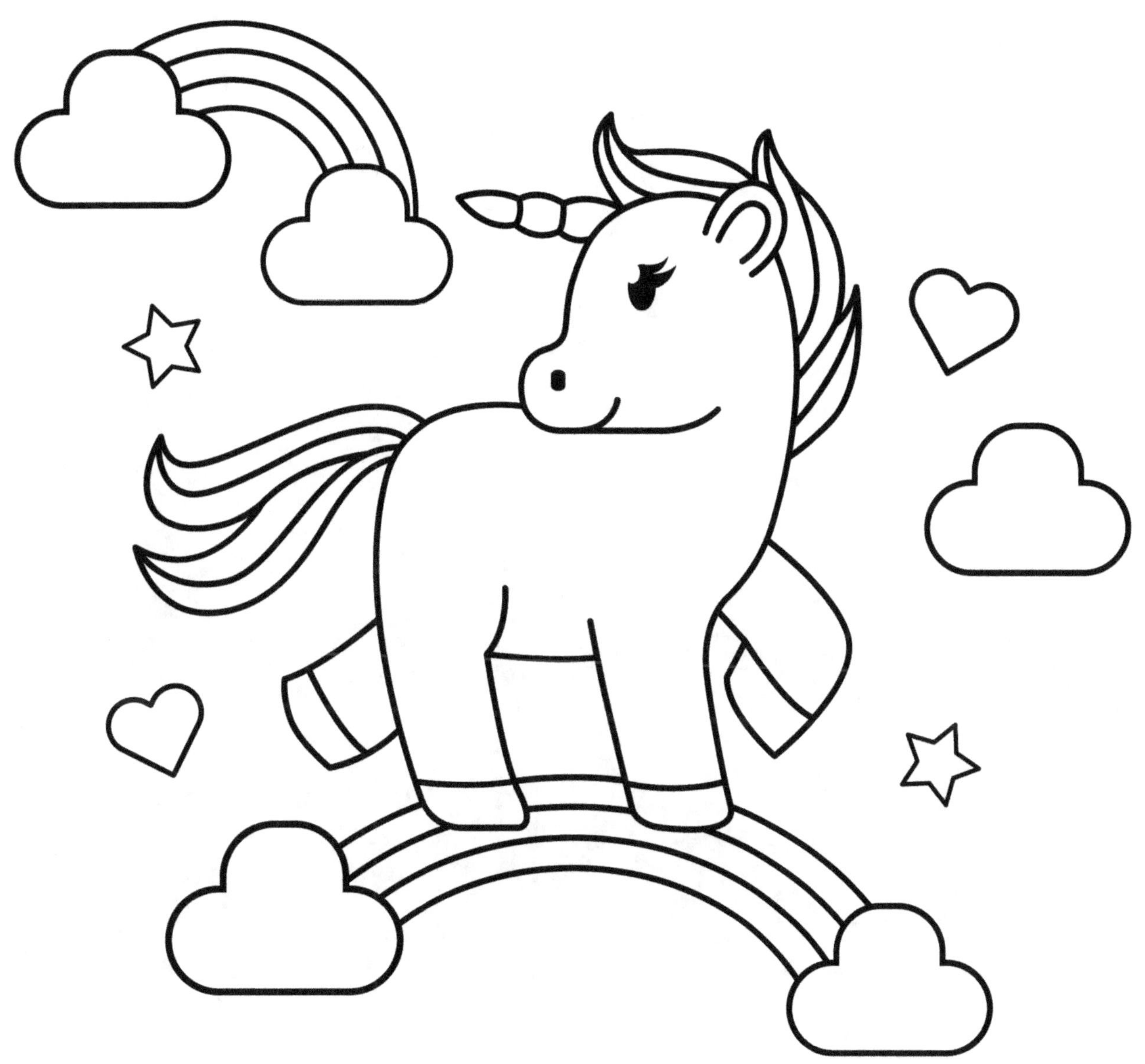

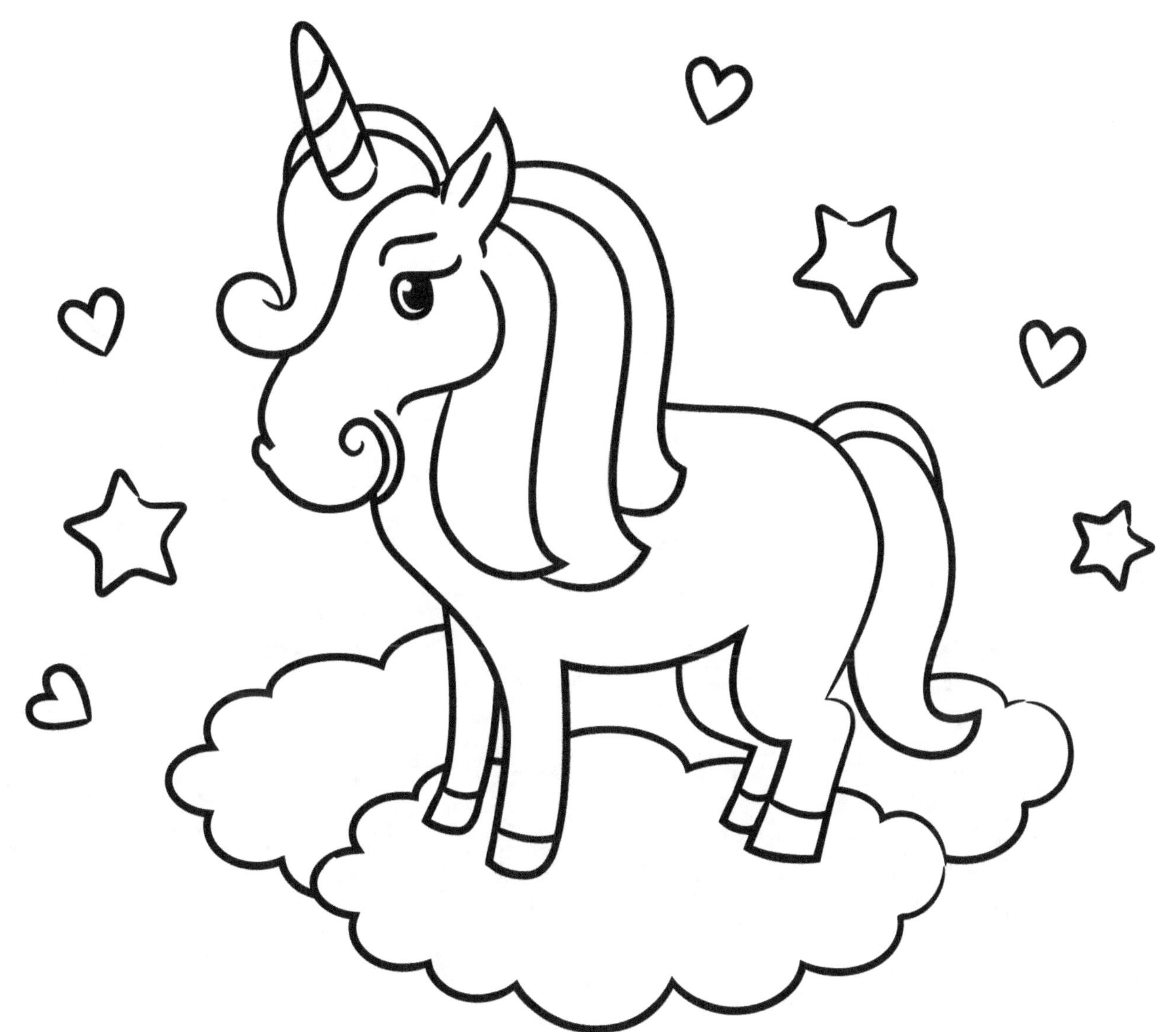

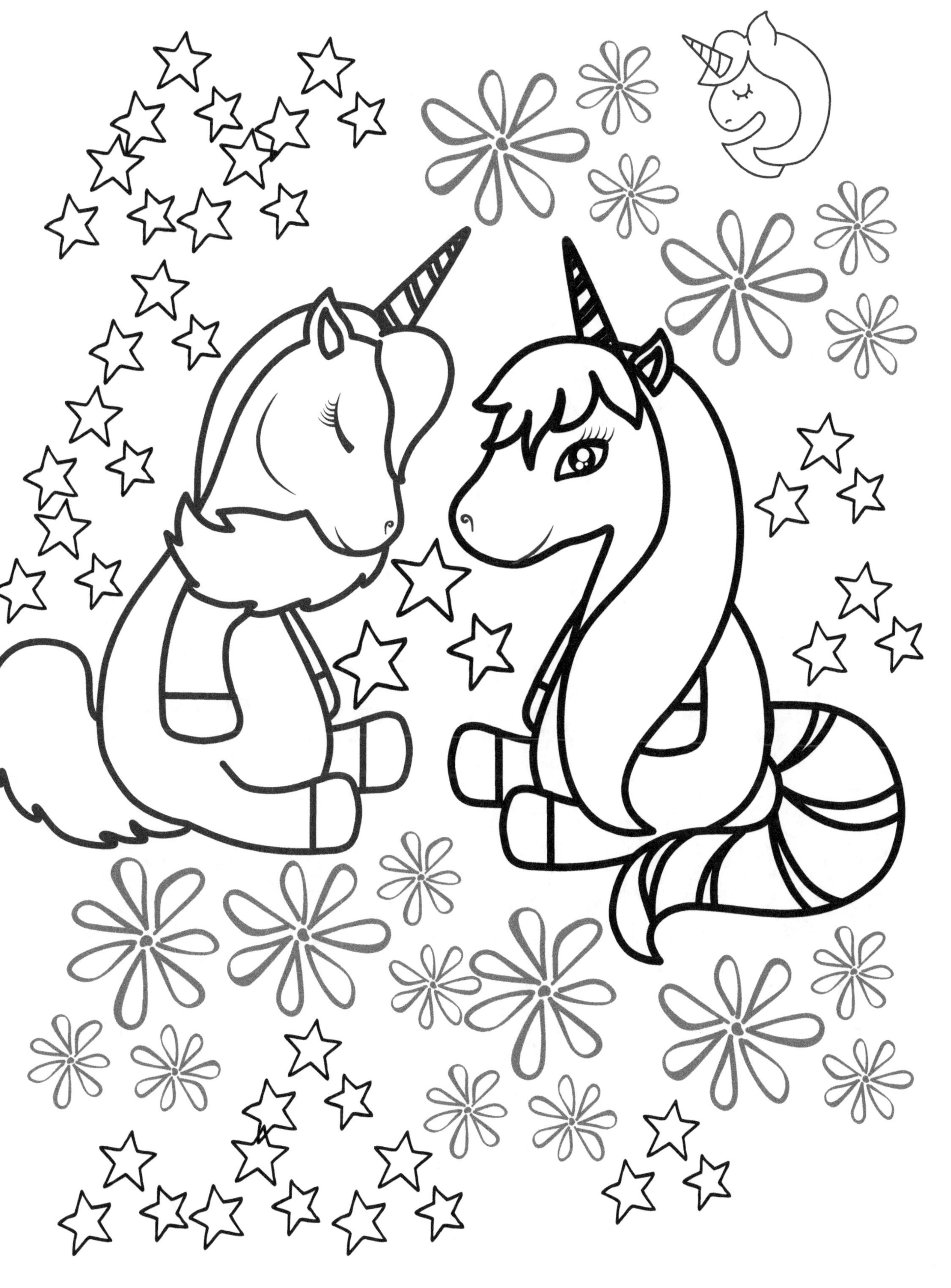

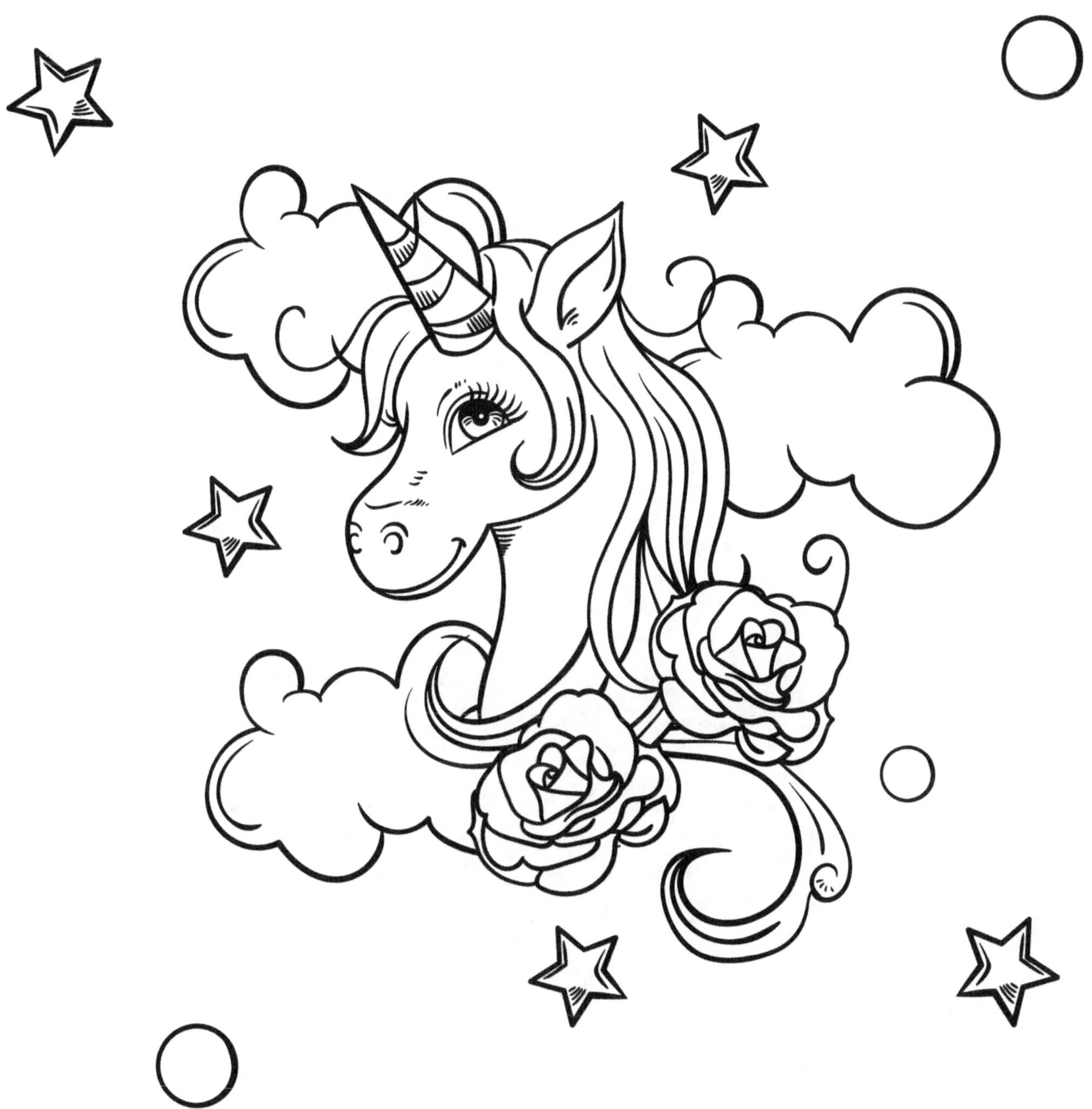

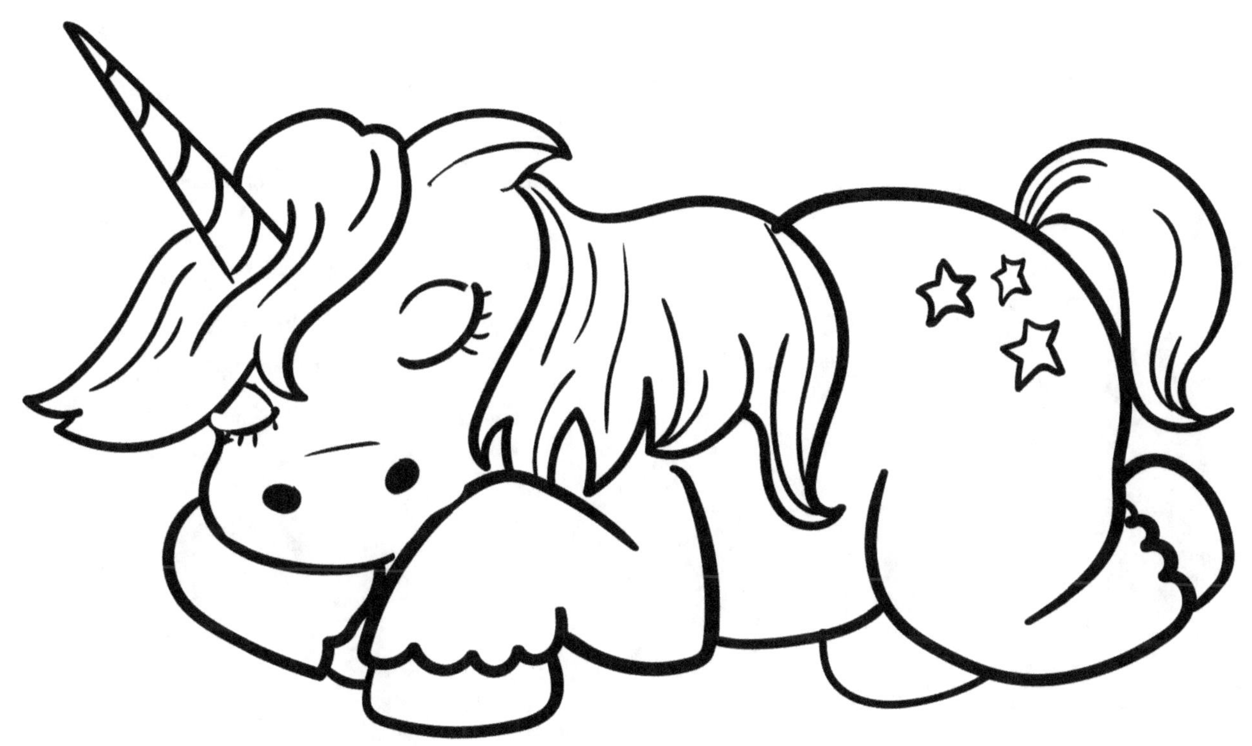